lalala

CROCHET
Amigurumi

15 Different Amigurumi Projects to Crochet

María Alejandra Montero

Tuva Publishing

www.tuvayayincilik.com

Address: Merkez Mah. Cavusbasi Cad. No:71
Cekmekoy / Istanbul 34782 Turkey
Tel: +9 0216 642 62 62

Crochet Amigurumi

First Print: 2014 / March
Second Print: 2015 / January

All Global Copyrights Belongs To
Tuva Tekstil San. ve Dış Tic. Ltd. Şti.

Content: Crochet

Editor in Chief: Ayhan DEMİRPEHLİVAN
Project Editor: Kader DEMİRPEHLİVAN
Designer: María Alejandra Montero
Text Editor: Zoë HALSTEAD
Technical Advisor: K. Leyla ARAS
Graphic Design: Jorge PENNY, Ömer ALP

ISBN: 978-605-5647-56-8

Printing House
Bilnet Matbaacılık - Biltur Yayın ve Hizmet A.Ş. Dudullu
Organize Sanayi Bolgesi 1. Cadde No:16 - Umraniye - Istanbul / Turkey

ACKNOWLEDGEMENTS

To my grandmother Isabel, who gave me my first crochet hook and from whom I inherited this obsession.

 facebook.com/TuvaYayincilik

 twitter.com/TuvaYayincilik

 pinterest.com/TuvaPublishing

CONTENTS

PROJECTS

WELCOME

Amigurumi is the Japanese art of crocheting small stuffed animals and dolls. Making an amigurumi is an enjoyable and fun activity and not at all complicated or tedious. With patience and time you will be able to create toys and dolls that will become little friends.

You will learn to crochet the different parts of the toy, how to sew them together and add the features to bring the character to life. Once you have finished your first amigurumi a whole world of possibility will be opened up and your creativity can flow.

This book is a collection of toys all created using DMC Natura. The projects range in skill level from basic projects such as the Three Balls to more complex ones like A Happy Family. So sit down, get comfortable, make yourself a cup of tea and get ready to create lots of lovely toys and characters all handmade by you!

1

SYNTHETIC

8

MATERIALS

1 · DMC Natura
2 · Crochet hook:
    Size 3 mm (UK 11)
3 · Tapestry needles
4 · Sewing needles
5 · Pins
6 · Scissors
7 · Safety eyes and noses
    Optional:
    Buttons
    Felt
8 · Stuffing:
    Wool: compact
    Synthetic: softer

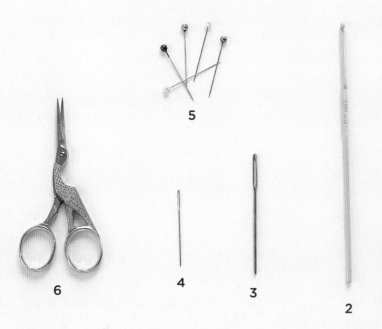

5

4

3

2

6

WOOL

Buttons or felt are good substitute
options for the safety eyes.

7

GETTING STARTED

MAGIC RING: The Magic Ring is the perfect technique for starting projects in the round.

Make a loop with the yarn.

Hold the loop where the yarn crosses over.

Insert hook into the loop from front to back.

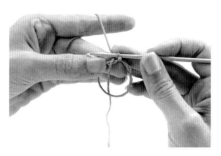

Wrap yarn round hook and pull through loop to front.

Repeat the last step so that you have 2 loops on hook. Yarn round hook and pull through both loops. Double crochet made.

Repeat until you have completed six double crochet stitches.

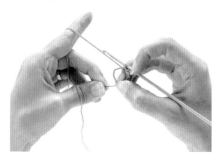

Take the tail of the yarn and pull to close the ring.

Insert the hook into the top of the first stitch worked and make a slip stitch to join the ring.

Now you have a completed magic ring!

CROCHET TECHNIQUES

CHAIN STITCH: With the slip knot on your hook, wrap yarn round hook and pull through loop.

 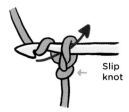

Slip knot

← 1 stitch

3 stitches

 DOUBLE CROCHET: Insert the hook into the stitch, wrap yarn round hook then pull it through. 2 loops on hook. Wrap yarn round hook again and pull through both loops. Double crochet stitch made.

 INCREASE: Make a double crochet stitch as before. Then insert your hook in the same place as the stitch just worked and make another double crochet stitch.

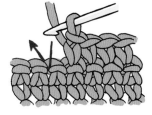 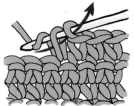

 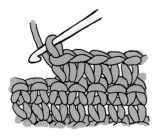

 DECREASE: Insert the hook into the first stitch, wrap yarn round hook and pull through. Then insert hook in next stitch along, wrap yarn round hook and pull through. 3 loops now on hook. Wrap yarn round hook again and pull through all 3 loops.

 SLIP STITCH: Insert the hook into the stitch, wrap yarn round hook and pull through both loops.

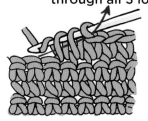 

Diagrams show the reverse side of the rows.

READING THE PATTERNS

For each part of your amigurumi, there are two different sets of crochet instructions to follow; a visual diagram or chart and an instructional list or formula. Knowing how to read each one and understanding the symbols used will help you complete your amigurumi easily.

CHART & FORMULA SYMBOLS

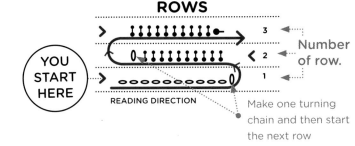

◎ MAGIC RING
● CHAIN STITCH
0 TURNING CHAIN
⁐ DOUBLE CROCHET
Y INCREASE
⅄ DECREASE
● SLIP STITCH

CHARTS

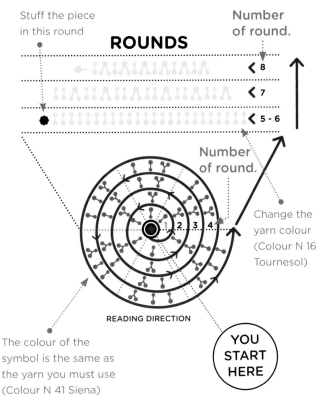

ROUNDS

Stuff the piece in this round

Number of round.

8
7
5 - 6

Number of round.

Change the yarn colour (Colour N 16 Tournesol)

READING DIRECTION

The colour of the symbol is the same as the yarn you must use (Colour N 41 Siena)

YOU START HERE

ROWS

3
2
1

Number of row.

YOU START HERE

READING DIRECTION

Make one turning chain and then start the next row

All the charts should be read from bottom to top.

To work in rounds: For example a ball or the leg of a doll; start at the centre of the circle and work outwards in a spiral, following the stitch instructions. When you reach the edge of the circle you have achieved the correct diameter. Next, follow the remaining instructions above the circle, working upwards according to the numbering.

To work in rows: Start in the lower left corner of the chart and work to the end of the line then turn. Follow the next line from right to left, then repeat until the end of the chart.

FORMULAS

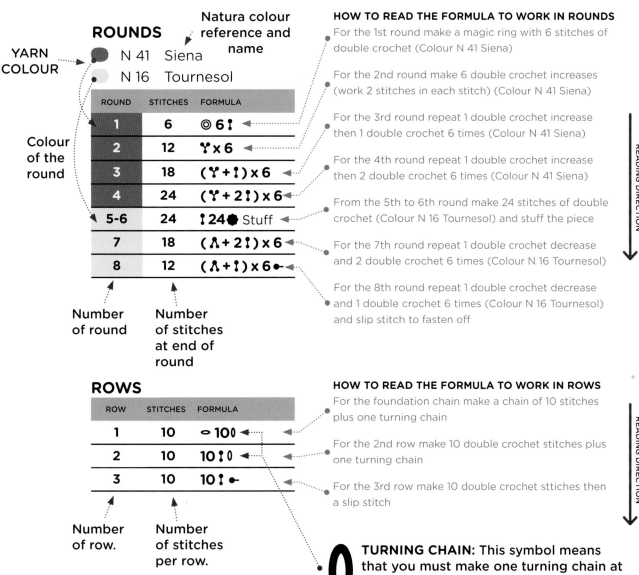

YARN COLOUR

ROUNDS

Natura colour reference and name

● N 41 Siena
○ N 16 Tournesol

Colour of the round

ROUND	STITCHES	FORMULA
1	6	◎ 6 ⚊
2	12	Y × 6
3	18	(Y + ⚊) × 6
4	24	(Y + 2⚊) × 6
5-6	24	⚊24● Stuff
7	18	(Λ + 2⚊) × 6
8	12	(Λ + ⚊) × 6 ●

Number of round

Number of stitches at end of round

HOW TO READ THE FORMULA TO WORK IN ROUNDS

For the 1st round make a magic ring with 6 stitches of double crochet (Colour N 41 Siena)

For the 2nd round make 6 double crochet increases (work 2 stitches in each stitch) (Colour N 41 Siena)

For the 3rd round repeat 1 double crochet increase then 1 double crochet 6 times (Colour N 41 Siena)

For the 4th round repeat 1 double crochet increase then 2 double crochet 6 times (Colour N 41 Siena)

From the 5th to 6th round make 24 stitches of double crochet (Colour N 16 Tournesol) and stuff the piece

For the 7th round repeat 1 double crochet decrease and 2 double crochet 6 times (Colour N 16 Tournesol)

For the 8th round repeat 1 double crochet decrease and 1 double crochet 6 times (Colour N 16 Tournesol) and slip stitch to fasten off

READING DIRECTION

ROWS

ROW	STITCHES	FORMULA
1	10	○ 10 0
2	10	10 ⚊ 0
3	10	10 ⚊ ●

Number of row.

Number of stitches per row.

HOW TO READ THE FORMULA TO WORK IN ROWS

For the foundation chain make a chain of 10 stitches plus one turning chain

For the 2nd row make 10 double crochet stitches plus one turning chain

For the 3rd row make 10 double crochet sttiches then a slip stitch

READING DIRECTION

0 TURNING CHAIN: This symbol means that you must make one turning chain at the end of your row to achieve the right height for your next row of stitches.

9

EYES AND NOSES

There are many options for adding features:

Safety eyes and noses
These are safe for children and can be bought in craft stores and the internet. Insert the post of the eye or nose through the crochet fabric in the correct position. Push the washer onto the post on the reverse and click into place.

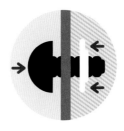

Attaching the nose

Buttons
Buttons are a quick and easy way to add that final touch to your amigurumi. You can use them as eyes or noses.

Transparent safety eye

Button

Felt
You can also use felt to add features to your amigurumi. Cut the felt to the desired shape then sew to the toy's face in the correct position.

Felt

Embroidery

Embroidery
Embroidery allows you to add more delicate detail and expression to your amigurumi.

STUFFING

The amigurumi's final appearance depends on how much stuffing you put into each pieces.

In fixed parts

In moveable parts

How to make moveable parts

If you want the arms and legs to move; stuff down into the tips only, leaving towards the top empty. Oversew the top edges then sew to toy.

How to make fixed parts

If you want fixed legs and arms, stuff pieces completely and attach them to the body using an oversew stitch.

ASSEMBLING

First pin all of the parts in position. Then, using a tapestry needle and matching yarn, oversew each part together.

TIP: Make evenly spaced diagonal stitches.

HIDING YARN ENDS

1

1. Thread the yarn end onto a tapestry needle.

2

3

2. Insert the needle into the amigurumi and pull it out on the other side of the part.

3. Pull tight then snip off the excess yarn.

CORRECT SIDE

Please note that all the crochet pieces have a right (correct) side and a wrong (reverse) side. In these photos you can clearly see the difference between the two.

Front side (right)

Reverse side (wrong)

CROCHET HOOK SIZES

Metric size	UK	US	JAPAN
2.25 mm	13	B / 1	3/0
2.50 mm	12	-	4/0
2.75 mm	-	C / 2	-
3 mm	11	-	5/0
3.25 mm	10	D / 3	-
3.50 mm	9	E / 4	6/0
3.75 mm	-	F / 5	-
4 mm	8	G / 6	7/0
4.50 mm	7	7	-
5 mm	6	H / 8	8/0
5.5 mm	5	I / 9	-
6 mm	4	J / 10	10/0
6.5 mm	3	K / 10 1/2	-
7 mm	2	-	-
8 mm	0	L / 11	-
9 mm	00	M / 13	-
10 mm	000	N / 15	-

GLOSSARY AND ABBREVIATIONS

UK	US
Chain (ch)	Chain (ch)
Double crochet (dc)	Single crochet (sc)
Treble (tr)	Double crochet (dc)
Half treble (htr)	Half double crochet (hdc)
Double treble (dtr)	Triple crochet (trc)
Slip stitch (sl st)	Slip stitch (sl sc)

THREE BALLS
FOR PLAY

This is an easy and fun first step to making amigurumi!

YARNS:

DMC NATURA

- N 61   Crimson
- N 03   Sable
- N 13   Pistache
- N 34   Bourgogne
- N 20   Jade
- N 59   Prune
- N 76   Lima

MATERIALS:

· Stuffing

TOOLS:

· 3 mm crochet hook

· Tapestry needle

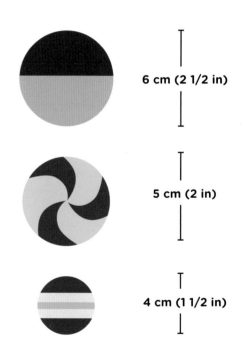

6 cm (2 1/2 in)

5 cm (2 in)

4 cm (1 1/2 in)

THREE BALLS

HOW TO CROCHET

Always start with a magic ring of 6 stitches. Work in rounds.

CHART SYMBOLS

- ◎ MAGIC RING
- ⬭ CHAIN STITCH
- 0 TURNING CHAIN
- ⬩ DOUBLE CROCHET
- Y INCREASE
- ⋏ DECREASE
- ⬩⬤ SLIP STITCH

Ⓐ BALL 1

- ⬤ N 61   Crimson
- ⬤ N 03   Sable
- ⬤ N 13   Pistache

ROUND	STITCHES	FORMULA
1	6	◎ 6 $\mathbf{I}$
2	12	Y × 6
3	18	(Y + $\mathbf{I}$) × 6
4	24	(Y + 2$\mathbf{I}$) × 6
5	30	(Y + 3$\mathbf{I}$) × 6
6	30	$\mathbf{I}$ 30
7	30	$\mathbf{I}$ 30
8	30	$\mathbf{I}$ 30
9	24	(⋏ + 3$\mathbf{I}$) × 6
10	18	(⋏ + 2$\mathbf{I}$) × 6 ⬤ Stuff
11	12	(⋏ + $\mathbf{I}$) × 6
12	6	⋏ × 6 ⬩⬤

BALL 1

Ⓑ BALL 2

■ N 34 Bourgogne
● N 20 Jade

ROUND	STITCHES	FORMULA
1	6	◎ 6 !
2	12	Y × 6
3	18	(Y + !) × 6
4	24	(Y + 2!) × 6
5	30	(Y + 3!) × 6
6	36	(Y + 4!) × 6
7	42	(Y + 5!) × 6
8	48	(Y + 6!) × 6
9-11	48	! 48
12-14	48	! 48
15	42	(Λ + 6!) × 6
16	36	(Λ + 5!) × 6
17	30	(Λ + 4!) × 6
18	24	(Λ + 3!) × 6
19	18	(Λ + 2!) × 6 ● Stuff
20	12	(Λ + !) × 6
21	6	Λ × 6 ●

BALL 2

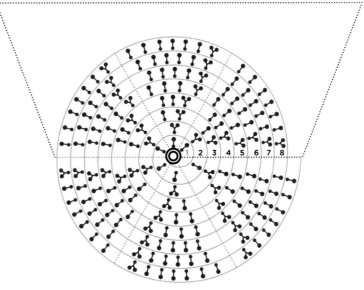

21
20
19 ●
18
17
16
15
12-14
9-11

Ⓒ BALL 3

● N 59 Prune
● N 76 Lima

ROUND	STITCHES	FORMULA
1	6	◎ ! ● + ! ● × 3
2	12	Y ● + Y ● × 3
3	18	(Y + ! ●) + (Y + ! ●) × 3
4	24	(Y + 2 ! ●) + (Y + 2 ! ●) × 3
5	30	(Y + 3 ! ●) + (Y + 3 ! ●) × 3
6	36	(Y + 4 ! ●) + (Y + 4 ! ●) × 3
7	42	(Y + 5 ! ●) + (Y + 5 ! ●) × 3
8-12	42	7 ! ● + 7 ! ● × 3
13	36	(Λ + 5 ! ●) + (Λ + 5 ! ●) × 3
14	30	(Λ + 4 ! ●) + (Λ + 4 ! ●) × 3
15	24	(Λ + 3 ! ●) + (Λ + 3 ! ●) × 3
16	18	(Λ + 2 ! ●) + (Λ + 2 ! ●) × 3 ✿ Stuff
17	12	(Λ + ! ●) + (Λ + ! ●) × 3
18	6	Λ ● + Λ ● × 3 ➤

BALL 3

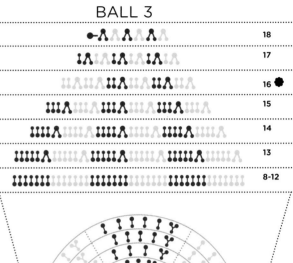

5

ASSEMBLING AND DETAILS

1. Start with a magic ring of 6 stitches.

2. Make the ball changing colour as instructed.

3. Close the ball once stuffed.

4. Hide the excess of yarn

6

HOW TO CLOSE A BALL

7-8

5. Thread the yarn end onto a needle then insert the needle through all of the outer loops of the final round.

6. Pull the yarn to close the hole.

7. Insert the needle into the centre of the final round and bring it out on the other side of the ball.

8. Snip off the excess yarn.

9

COLOURED STACKER
PLAY AND LEARN

Make this classic toy to help your little ones learn their colours and have lots of fun.

YARNS:

DMC NATURA

	N 35	Nacar
⬤	N 62	Cerise
⬤	N 16	Tournesol
⬤	N 13	Pistache
⬤	N 49	Turquoise

MATERIALS:

· Stuffing

· Felt

· Cardboard tube from paper towels

TOOLS:

· 3 mm crochet hook

· Tapestry needle

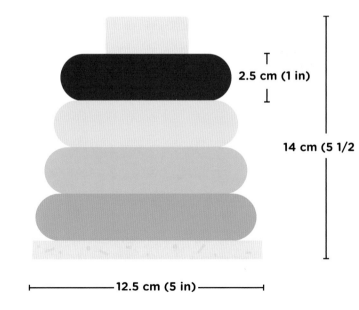

2.5 cm (1 in)

14 cm (5 1/2

12.5 cm (5 in)

COLOURED STACKER

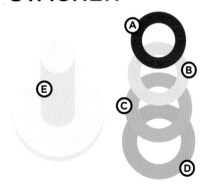

HOW TO CROCHET

Make chains and join to form a ring. Work in rounds.

CHART SYMBOLS

- ◎ MAGIC RING
- ● CHAIN STITCH
- 0 TURNING CHAIN
- ⬤ DOUBLE CROCHET
- Y INCREASE
- Λ DECREASE
- ● SLIP STITCH

(A) HOOP A

● N 62 Cerise

Start by making a chain of 42 stiches

ROUND	STITCHES	FORMULA
1	42	○ 42 ●
2-3	42	⬤ 42
4	48	(Y + 6⬤) × 6
5	54	(Y + 7⬤) × 6
6	60	(Y + 8⬤) × 6
7	66	(Y + 9⬤) × 6
8-11	66	⬤ 66
12	60	(Λ + 9⬤) × 6
13	54	(Λ + 8⬤) × 6
14	48	(Λ + 7⬤) × 6
15	42	(Λ + 6⬤) × 6
16	42	⬤ 42
17	42	⬤ 42 ●

HOOP

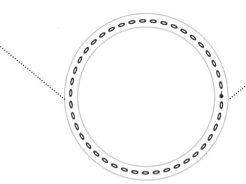

●—⬤⬤	17
⬤⬤	16
⬤⬤⬤⬤⬤⬤Λ⬤⬤⬤⬤⬤⬤Λ⬤⬤⬤⬤⬤⬤Λ⬤⬤⬤⬤⬤⬤Λ⬤⬤⬤⬤⬤⬤Λ⬤⬤⬤⬤⬤⬤Λ	15
⬤⬤⬤⬤⬤⬤⬤Λ⬤⬤⬤⬤⬤⬤⬤Λ⬤⬤⬤⬤⬤⬤⬤Λ⬤⬤⬤⬤⬤⬤⬤Λ⬤⬤⬤⬤⬤⬤⬤Λ⬤⬤⬤⬤⬤⬤⬤Λ	14
⬤⬤⬤⬤⬤⬤⬤⬤Λ⬤⬤⬤⬤⬤⬤⬤⬤Λ⬤⬤⬤⬤⬤⬤⬤⬤Λ⬤⬤⬤⬤⬤⬤⬤⬤Λ⬤⬤⬤⬤⬤⬤⬤⬤Λ	13
⬤⬤⬤⬤⬤⬤⬤⬤⬤Λ⬤⬤⬤⬤⬤⬤⬤⬤⬤Λ⬤⬤⬤⬤⬤⬤⬤⬤⬤Λ⬤⬤⬤⬤⬤⬤⬤⬤⬤Λ⬤⬤⬤⬤⬤⬤⬤⬤⬤Λ	12
⬤⬤	8-11
⬤⬤⬤⬤⬤⬤⬤Y⬤⬤⬤⬤⬤⬤⬤Y⬤⬤⬤⬤⬤⬤⬤Y⬤⬤⬤⬤⬤⬤⬤Y⬤⬤⬤⬤⬤⬤⬤Y⬤⬤⬤⬤⬤⬤⬤Y	7
⬤⬤⬤⬤⬤⬤⬤Y⬤⬤⬤⬤⬤⬤Y⬤⬤⬤⬤⬤⬤Y⬤⬤⬤⬤⬤⬤Y⬤⬤⬤⬤⬤⬤Y⬤⬤⬤⬤⬤⬤Y	6
⬤⬤⬤⬤⬤⬤Y⬤⬤⬤⬤⬤Y⬤⬤⬤⬤⬤Y⬤⬤⬤⬤⬤Y⬤⬤⬤⬤⬤Y⬤⬤⬤⬤⬤Y	5
⬤⬤⬤⬤⬤Y⬤⬤⬤⬤Y⬤⬤⬤⬤Y⬤⬤⬤⬤Y⬤⬤⬤⬤Y⬤⬤⬤⬤Y	4
⬤⬤⬤⬤⬤⬤⬤⬤⬤⬤⬤⬤⬤⬤⬤⬤⬤⬤⬤⬤⬤⬤⬤⬤⬤⬤⬤⬤⬤⬤⬤⬤⬤⬤⬤⬤	2-3

Ⓑ HOOP B

N 16   Tournesol

Start by making a chain of 48 stiches

ROUND	STITCHES	FORMULA
1	48	⌒ 48 •─
2-3	48	❗ 48
4	54	(Ƴ + 7❗) × 6
5	60	(Ƴ + 8❗) × 6
6	66	(Ƴ + 9❗) × 6
7	72	(Ƴ + 10❗) × 6
8-11	72	❗ 72
12	66	(Λ + 10❗) × 6
13	60	(Λ + 9❗) × 6
14	54	(Λ + 8❗) × 6
15	48	(Λ + 7❗) × 6
16	48	❗ 48
17	48	❗ 48 •─

HOOP B

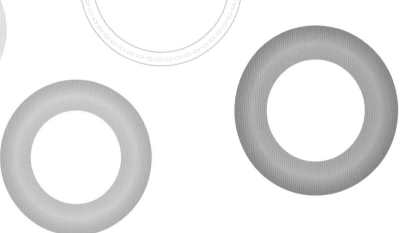

© HOOP C

🔵 N 13   Pistache

Start by making a chain of 54 stitches

ROUND	STITCHES	FORMULA
1	54	⬭ 54 •—
2-3	54	⌇ 54
4	60	(Y + 8⌇) × 6
5	66	(Y + 9⌇) × 6
6	72	(Y + 10⌇) × 6
7	78	(Y + 11⌇) × 6
8-11	78	⌇ 78
12	72	(Λ + 11⌇) × 6
13	66	(Λ + 10⌇) × 6
14	60	(Λ + 9⌇) × 6
15	54	(Λ + 8⌇) × 6
16	54	⌇ 54
17	54	⌇ 54 •—

HOOP C

●—⌇⌇⌇	17
⌇⌇⌇	16
⌇⌇⌇⌇⌇⌇⌇Λ⌇⌇⌇⌇⌇⌇⌇⌇Λ⌇⌇⌇⌇⌇⌇⌇⌇Λ⌇⌇⌇⌇⌇⌇⌇⌇Λ⌇⌇⌇⌇⌇⌇⌇⌇Λ⌇⌇⌇⌇⌇⌇⌇⌇Λ	15
⌇⌇⌇⌇⌇⌇⌇⌇Λ⌇⌇⌇⌇⌇⌇⌇⌇Λ⌇⌇⌇⌇⌇⌇⌇⌇Λ⌇⌇⌇⌇⌇⌇⌇⌇Λ⌇⌇⌇⌇⌇⌇⌇⌇Λ⌇⌇⌇⌇⌇⌇⌇⌇Λ	14
⌇⌇⌇⌇⌇⌇⌇⌇Λ⌇⌇⌇⌇⌇⌇⌇⌇⌇Λ⌇⌇⌇⌇⌇⌇⌇⌇⌇Λ⌇⌇⌇⌇⌇⌇⌇⌇⌇Λ⌇⌇⌇⌇⌇⌇⌇⌇⌇Λ⌇⌇⌇⌇⌇⌇⌇⌇⌇Λ	13
⌇⌇⌇⌇⌇⌇⌇⌇⌇⌇Λ⌇⌇⌇⌇⌇⌇⌇⌇⌇⌇Λ⌇⌇⌇⌇⌇⌇⌇⌇⌇⌇Λ⌇⌇⌇⌇⌇⌇⌇⌇⌇⌇Λ⌇⌇⌇⌇⌇⌇⌇⌇⌇⌇Λ	12
⌇⌇⌇	8-11
⌇⌇⌇⌇⌇⌇⌇⌇⌇V⌇⌇⌇⌇⌇⌇⌇⌇⌇V⌇⌇⌇⌇⌇⌇⌇⌇⌇V⌇⌇⌇⌇⌇⌇⌇⌇⌇V⌇⌇⌇⌇⌇⌇⌇⌇⌇V⌇⌇⌇⌇⌇⌇⌇⌇⌇V	7
⌇⌇⌇⌇⌇⌇⌇⌇V⌇⌇⌇⌇⌇⌇⌇⌇⌇V⌇⌇⌇⌇⌇⌇⌇⌇V⌇⌇⌇⌇⌇⌇⌇⌇V⌇⌇⌇⌇⌇⌇⌇⌇⌇V⌇⌇⌇⌇⌇⌇⌇⌇V	6
⌇⌇⌇⌇⌇⌇⌇V⌇⌇⌇⌇⌇⌇⌇⌇V⌇⌇⌇⌇⌇⌇⌇V⌇⌇⌇⌇⌇⌇⌇⌇V⌇⌇⌇⌇⌇⌇⌇V⌇⌇⌇⌇⌇⌇⌇⌇V	5
⌇⌇⌇⌇⌇⌇⌇V⌇⌇⌇⌇⌇⌇V⌇⌇⌇⌇⌇⌇⌇V⌇⌇⌇⌇⌇⌇V⌇⌇⌇⌇⌇⌇⌇V⌇⌇⌇⌇⌇⌇V	4
⌇⌇⌇	2-3

HOOP D

D HOOP D

⬤ N 49 Turquoise

Start by making a chain of 60 stitches

ROUND	STITCHES	FORMULA
1	60	⌒ **60** ←
2-3	60	❢ **60**
4	66	(Y + 9❢) × 6
5	72	(Y + 10❢) × 6
6	78	(Y + 11❢) × 6
7	84	(Y + 12❢) × 6
8-11	84	❢ **84**
12	78	(Λ + 12❢) × 6
13	72	(Λ + 11❢) × 6
14	66	(Λ + 10❢) × 6
15	60	(Λ + 9❢) × 6
16	60	❢ **60**
17	60	❢ **60** ←

HOOP D

```
17
16
15
14
13
12
8-11
7
6
5
4
2-3
```

Ⓔ TUBE

N 35 Nacar

ROUND	STITCHES	FORMULA
1	6	◎ 6 !
2	12	Y x 6
3	18	(Y + !) x 6
4	24	(Y + 2 !) x 6
5	30	(Y + 3 !) x 6
6-24	30	30 !
25	24	30 ! •-

TUBE

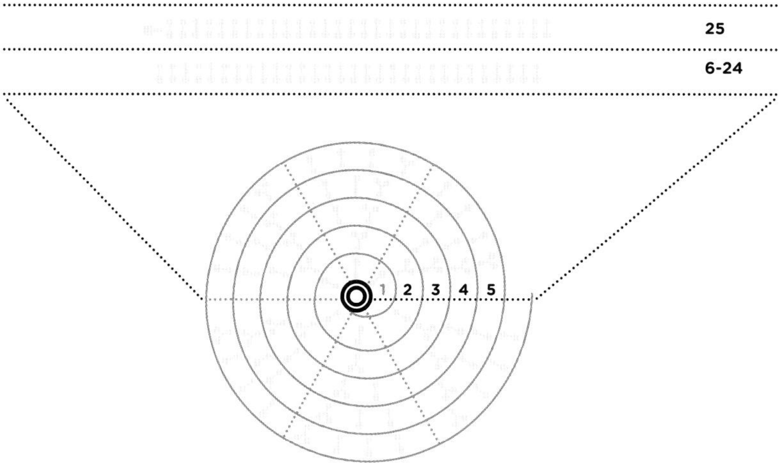

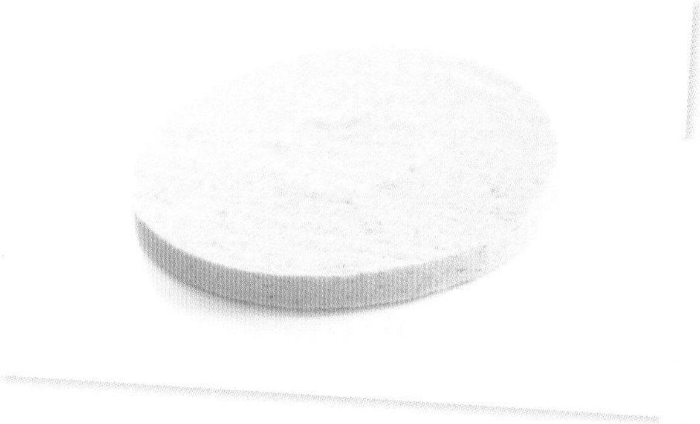

To make the base of the tube we used a felt circle 12.5cm (5 in) in diameter and 1cm (3/8 in) thick.

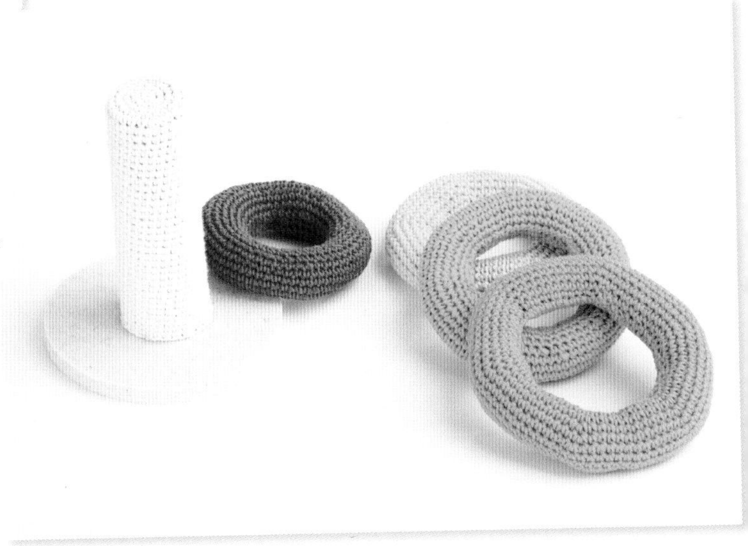

ASSEMBLING THE PARTS AND DETAILS

1. Once you have finished all the hoops, stuff and close them as shown on the previous pages.

2. Cut the cardboard tube to 12.5cm (5 in) in length.

3. Cut a circle of felt 12.5cm (5 in) in diameter.

4. Place the tube on the felt circle and draw around the base.

5. Place the cardboard tube inside the crochet tube.

6. Sit the tube on top of the felt, where marked, and sew through the felt base to secure.

7. Place the finished hoops on the tube.

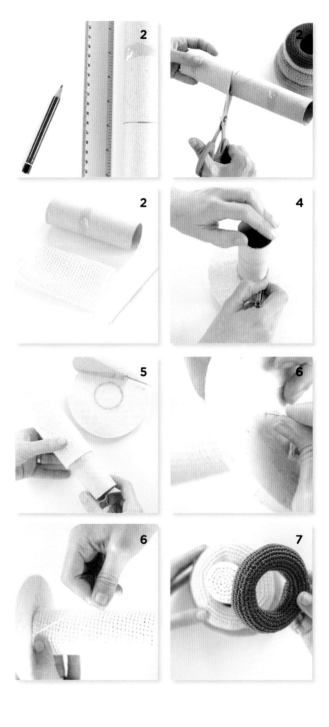

LARRY
THE TEDDY BEAR

He loves you, he just wants a hug, he is a tiny teddy bear and HIS NAME IS LARRY!

YARNS:

DMC NATURA
- N 41   Siena
- N 44   Agatha
- N 11   Noir

MATERIALS:
· 1 Pair of black safety eyes 9mm
· 1 Black nose 9 mm
· Stuffing

TOOLS:
· 3 mm crochet hook
· Tapestry needle

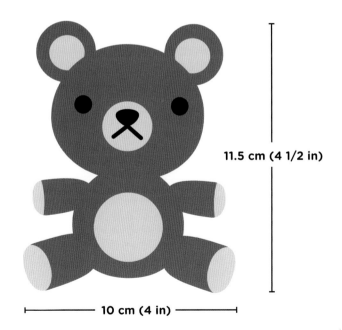

11.5 cm (4 1/2 in)

10 cm (4 in)

LARRY

HOW TO CROCHET

Always start with a magic ring of 6 stitches. Work in rounds and finish all the parts of your amigurumi before stuffing them and adding the face details.

CHART SYMBOLS

◎ MAGIC RING
● CHAIN STITCH
0 TURNING CHAIN
❗ DOUBLE CROCHET
Y INCREASE
⅄ DECREASE
● SLIP STITCH

Ⓐ HEAD
N 41 Siena

ROUND	STITCHES	FORMULA
1	6	◎ 6❗
2	12	Y × 6
3	18	(Y + ❗) × 6
4	24	(Y + 2❗) × 6
5	30	(Y + 3❗) × 6
6	36	(Y + 4❗) × 6
7	42	(Y + 5❗) × 6
8	48	(Y + 6❗) × 6
9	54	(Y + 7❗) × 6
10	60	(Y + 8❗) × 6
11-16	60	❗60
17	54	(⅄ + 8❗) × 6
18	48	(⅄ + 7❗) × 6
19	42	(⅄ + 6❗) × 6
20	36	(⅄ + 5❗) × 6
21	30	(⅄ + 4❗) × 6
22	24	(⅄ + 3❗) × 6 ●

HEAD

22
21
20
19
18
17
11 - 16

1 2 3 4 5 6 7 8 9 10

BODY

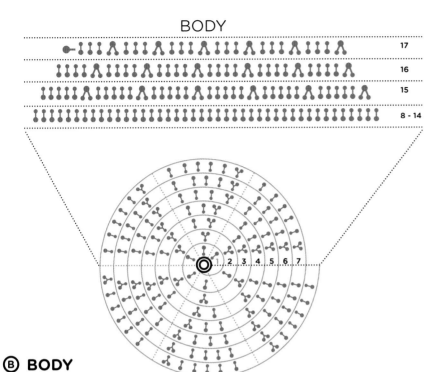

17
16
15
8 - 14

2 3 4 5 6 7

BELLY

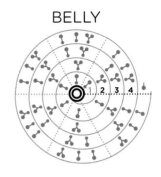

2 3 4

Ⓓ **BELLY**

N 44   Agatha

ROUND	STITCHES	FORMULA
1	6	◎ 6 !
2	12	Ƴ × 6
3	18	(Ƴ + !) × 6
4	24	(Ƴ + 2 !) × 6 ←

Ⓑ **BODY**

N 41   Siena

ROUND	STITCHES	FORMULA
1	6	◎ 6 !
2	12	Ƴ × 6
3	18	(Ƴ + !) × 6
4	24	(Ƴ + 2 !) × 6
5	30	(Ƴ + 3 !) × 6
6	36	(Ƴ + 4 !) × 6
7	42	(Ƴ + 5 !) × 6
8-14	42	! 42
15	36	(Λ + 5 !) × 6
16	30	(Λ + 4 !) × 6
17	24	(Λ + 3 !) × 6 ←

SNOUT

2 3

Ⓒ **SNOUT**

N 44   Agatha

ROUND	STITCHES	FORMULA
1	6	◎ 6 !
2	12	Ƴ × 6
3	18	(Ƴ + !) × 6 ←

Ⓔ ARM X 2

🔘 N 44 Agatha
⚫ N 41 Siena

ROUND	STITCHES	FORMULA
1	6	◎ 6 ¡
2	12	⋎ × 6
3-9	12	¡ 12
10	12	¡ 12 ⬤━

Ⓕ LEG X 2

🔘 N 44 Agatha
⚫ N 41 Siena

ROUND	STITCHES	FORMULA
1	6	◎ 6 ¡
2	12	⋎ × 6
3	18	(⋎ + ¡) × 6
4-10	18	¡ 18
11	18	¡ 18 ⬤━

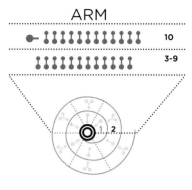

ARM

LEG

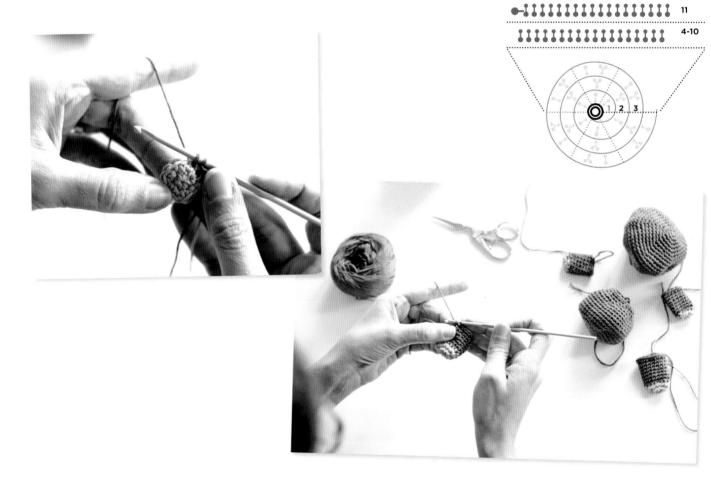

Ⓖ EAR (A) X 2

● N 41   Siena

ROUND	STITCHES	FORMULA
1	6	◎ 6 ❗
2	12	⋎ × 6
3	18	(⋎ + ❗) × 6
4	24	(⋎ + 2❗) × 6
5-6	24	❗24
7	18	(⋀ + 2❗) × 6
8	12	(⋀ + ❗) × 6 ●

Ⓗ EAR (B) X 2

○ N 44   Agatha

ROUND	STITCHES	FORMULA
1	6	◎ 6 ❗
2	12	⋎ × 6 ●

EAR (A)

EAR (B)

Press each ear in half and oversew bottom edges.

Sew each small circle to the centre of each ear.

35

ASSEMBLING THE PARTS AND DETAILS

1. Crochet all the parts.

2. Stuff the head, body and the legs. Then stuff the arms leaving the stuffing loose towards the top edges.

3. Attach the plastic nose to the snout circle. Embroider the mouth using N11 (Noir).

4. Sew the snout to the front of the head then attach the safety eyes.

5. Pin all the parts in position.

6. Sew the head onto the body. Then sew the belly circle to the body.

7. Sew the ears to the head.

8. Sew the legs to the body as shown.

9. Press the top edges of each arm together then oversew them. Sew to body in positions as shown.

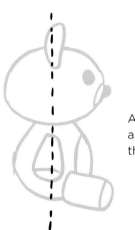

Align the arms with the ears

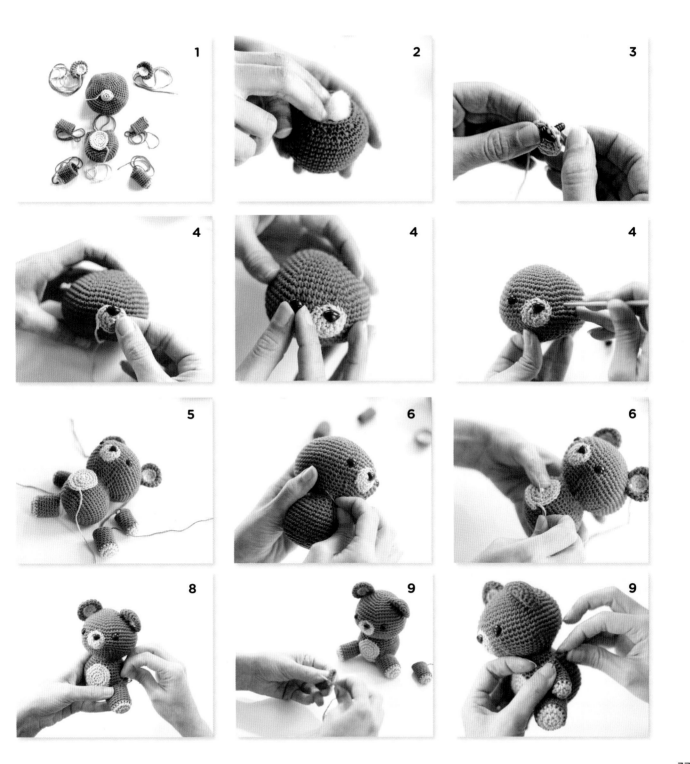

JIMBO
THE HUNGRY BUNNY

**He collects carrots to cook
a healthy soup.**

YARNS:

DMC NATURA

- N 38   Liquen
- N 01   Ibiza
- N 11   Noir
- N 51   Erica
- N 47   Safran
- N 48   Chartreuse

MATERIALS:

· 1 Pair of black safety eyes 9mm

· Stuffing

TOOLS:

· 3 mm crochet hook

· Tapestry needle

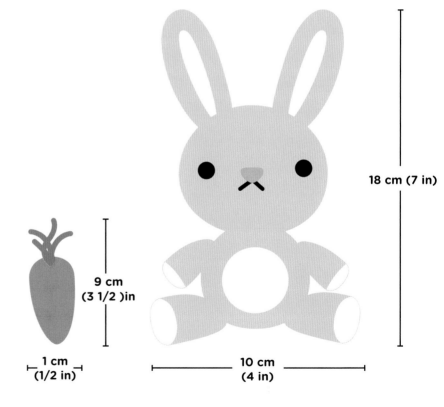

9 cm
(3 1/2)in

1 cm
(1/2 in)

18 cm (7 in)

10 cm
(4 in)

JIMBO

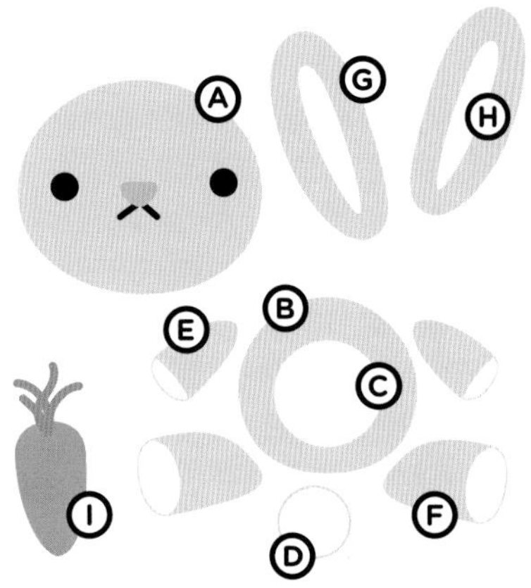

HOW TO CROCHET

Always start with a magic ring of 6 stitches. Work in rounds and finish all the parts of your amigurumi before stuffing them and adding the face details.

CHART SYMBOLS

◎ MAGIC RING
⬭ CHAIN STITCH
0 TURNING CHAIN
⫶ DOUBLE CROCHET
Y INCREASE
Λ DECREASE
•– SLIP STITCH

HEAD

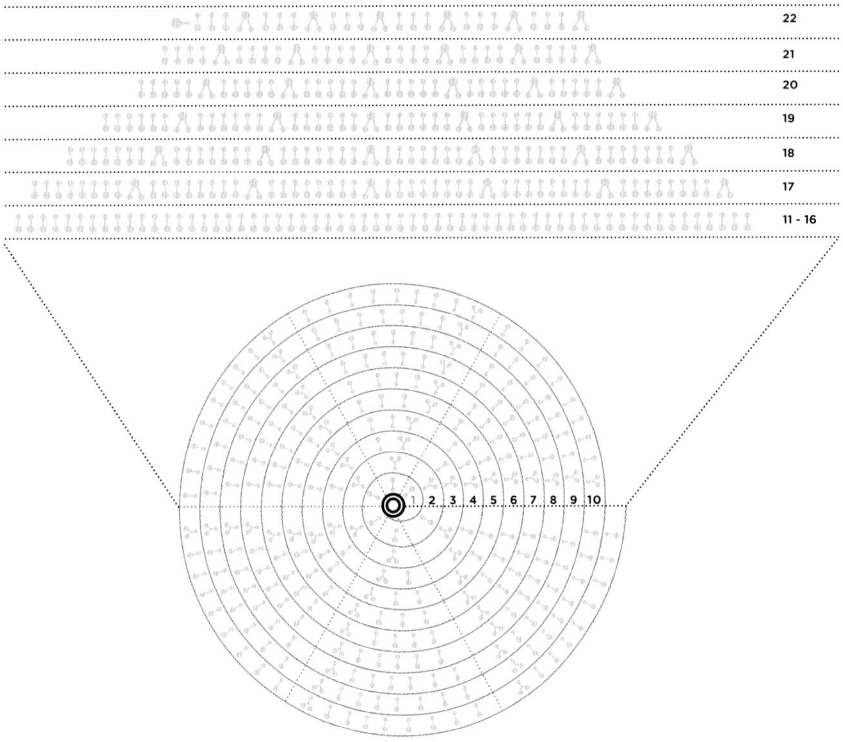

Ⓐ HEAD

N 38 Liquen

ROUND	STITCHES	FORMULA
1	6	◎ 6 ⫶
2	12	Y x 6
3	18	(Y + ⫶) x 6
4	24	(Y + 2 ⫶) x 6
5	30	(Y + 3 ⫶) x 6
6	36	(Y + 4 ⫶) x 6
7	42	(Y + 5 ⫶) x 6
8	48	(Y + 6 ⫶) x 6
9	54	(Y + 7 ⫶) x 6
10	60	(Y + 8 ⫶) x 6
11-16	60	⫶ 60
17	54	(Λ + 8 ⫶) x 6
18	48	(Λ + 7 ⫶) x 6
19	42	(Λ + 6 ⫶) x 6
20	36	(Λ + 5 ⫶) x 6
21	30	(Λ + 4 ⫶) x 6
22	24	(Λ + 3 ⫶) x 6 •–

Ⓑ BODY

N 38   Liquen

ROUND	STITCHES	FORMULA
1	6	◎ 6 !
2	12	Y × 6
3	18	(Y + !) × 6
4	24	(Y + 2 !) × 6
5	30	(Y + 3 !) × 6
6	36	(Y + 4 !) × 6
7	42	(Y + 5 !) × 6
8-14	42	! 42
15	36	(Λ + 5 !) × 6
16	30	(Λ + 4 !) × 6
17	24	(Λ + 3 !) × 6 ●

BODY

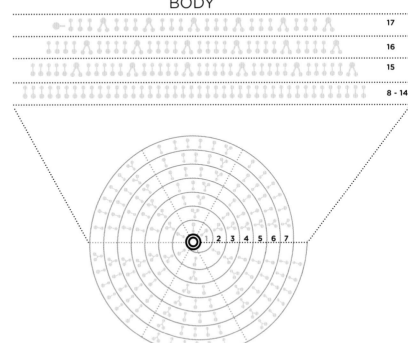

BELLY

Ⓒ BELLY

N 01   Ibiza

ROUND	STITCHES	FORMULA
1	6	◎ 6 !
2	12	Y × 6
3	18	(Y + !) × 6
4	24	(Y + 2 !) × 6 ●

TAIL

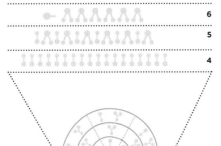

Ⓓ TAIL

N 38   Liquen

ROUND	STITCHES	FORMULA
1	6	◎ 6 !
2	12	Y × 6
3	18	(Y + !) × 6
4	18	! 18
5	12	(Λ + !) × 6
6	6	(Λ) × 6 ●

Ⓔ ARM X 2

⬤ N 38 Liquen
◯ N 01 Ibiza

ROUND	STITCHES	FORMULA
1	6	◎ 6 !
2	12	Y × 6
3-9	12	! 12
10	22	! 12 ←

Ⓕ LEG X 2

⬤ N 38 Liquen
◯ N 01 Ibiza

ROUND	STITCHES	FORMULA
1	6	◎ 6 !
2	12	Y × 6
3	18	(Y + !) × 6
4-10	18	! 18
11	18	! 18 ←

Ⓖ EAR (A) X 2

⬤ N 38 Liquen

ROUND	STITCHES	FORMULA
1	6	◎ 6 !
2	12	Y × 6
3	18	(Y + !) × 6
4-15	18	! 18
16	12	(⋀ + !) × 6
17	6	⋀ × 6 ←

ARM

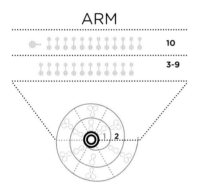

LEG

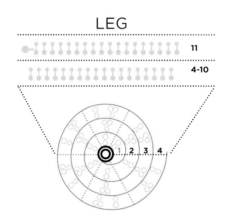

EAR (A)

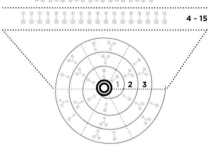

Ⓗ EAR (B) X 2

◯ N 01 Ibiza

ROW	STITCHES	FORMULA
1	10	↼ 10 0
2	10	10 ! ←

EAR (B)

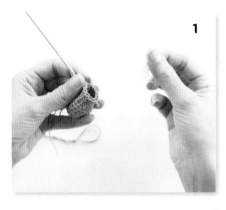

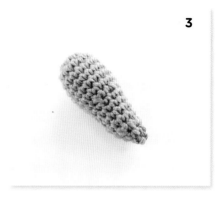

① CARROT

N 47   Safran

ROUND	STITCHES	FORMULA
1	6	◎ 6 ‼
2	12	⋎ × 6
3	18	(⋎ + ‼) × 6
4-7	18	‼ 18
8	12	(⋏ + ‼) × 6
9-12	12	‼ 12 ✿ Stuff
13	6	⋏ × 6
14	6	‼ 6 ●

CARROT

‼‼‼‼‼ **14**

⋏⋏⋏⋏⋏⋏ **13**

‼‼‼‼‼‼‼‼‼‼‼‼ **9-12** ✿

‼⋏‼⋏‼⋏‼⋏‼⋏‼⋏ **8**

‼‼‼‼‼‼‼‼‼‼‼‼‼‼‼‼‼‼ **4-7**

1. Stuff the carrot before completing it.

2. Work the remaining rounds to close it.

3. Now you have the main part of the carrot.

4. Thread a length of N48 (Chartreuse) onto a needle. Insert the needle in the top of the carrot, knot the yarn close to the carrot then cut the yarn to 2.5cm (1 in) long.

5. Repeat several times until you have the desired amount.

6. The finished carrot top.

43

ASSEMBLING THE PARTS AND DETAILS

1. Once you have crocheted all the parts, stuff the head and body. Then stuff the arms and legs leaving the stuffing loose towards the top edges.

2. Embroider a triangle shape of stitches using N51 (Erica). Then embroider the mouth using N11 (Noir).

3. Attach the safety eyes.

4. Flatten the ears then oversew the bottom edges. Sew the white inner ears (B) to the centre of each ear. Then pinch the bottom edges together and sew to secure as shown.

5. Sew the head onto the body. Then sew the belly circle to the body.

6. Press the top edges of the arms together and oversew. Sew to body in positions as shown. Repeat this process with the legs and sew to base of body as shown.

7. Sew the tail to the body as shown.

8. Pin the ears in place then sew them to the head.

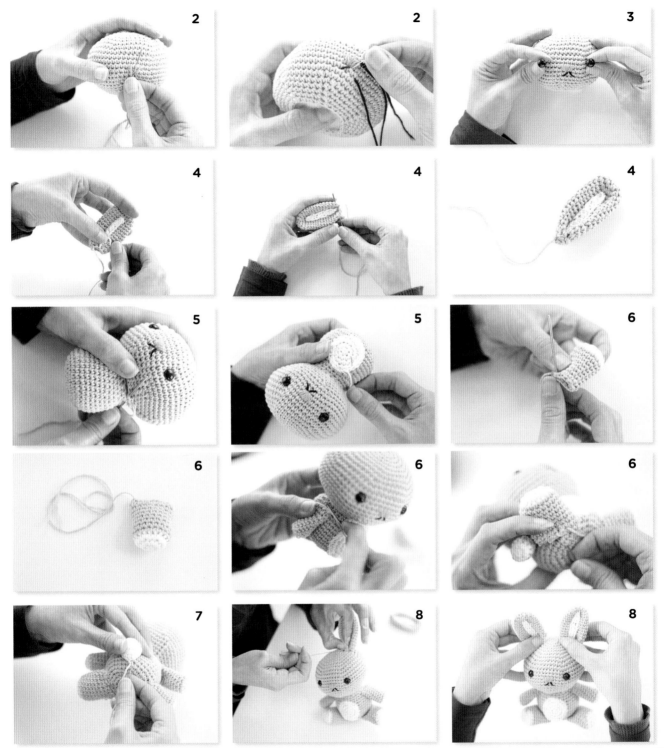

JOE & THE ROCKET
THE SPACE TRAVELLER

He lives in outer space occasionally going back down to earth to visit his mother.

YARNS:

DMC NATURA

- N 09 Gris Argent
- N 23 Passion
- N 64 Prussian
- N 28 Zaphire
- N 01 Ibiza
- N 47 Safran

MATERIALS:

· Stuffing

TOOLS:

· 3 mm crochet hook
· Tapestry needle

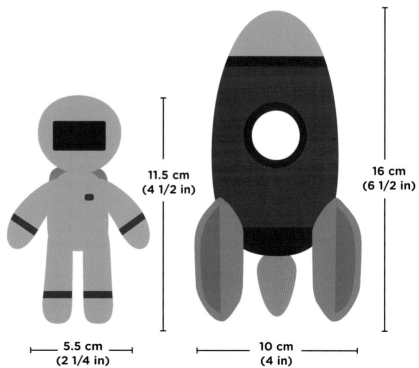

11.5 cm
(4 1/2 in)

16 cm
(6 1/2 in)

5.5 cm
(2 1/4 in)

10 cm
(4 in)

JOE

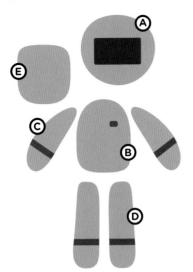

HOW TO CROCHET

Always start with a magic ring of 6 stitches. Work in rounds and finish all the parts of your amigurumi before stuffing them and adding the details.

CHART SYMBOLS

- ◎ MAGIC RING
- ➊ CHAIN STITCH
- ⓪ TURNING CHAIN
- ❗ DOUBLE CROCHET
- ❤ INCREASE
- ⋀ DECREASE
- ● SLIP STITCH

Ⓐ HEAD

- 🔘 N 09 Gris Argent
- ⚫ N 28 Zaphire

ROUND	STITCHES	FORMULA
1	6	◎ 6 ❗
2	12	❤ × 6
3	18	(❤ + ❗) × 6
4	24	(❤ + 2 ❗) × 6
5	30	(❤ + 3 ❗) × 6
6	36	(❤ + 4 ❗) × 6
7-10	36	8 ❗ ⚫ + 28 ❗ 🔘
11	30	(⋀ + 4 ❗) × 6
12	24	(⋀ + 3 ❗) × 6
13	18	(⋀ + 2 ❗) × 6 ●

HEAD

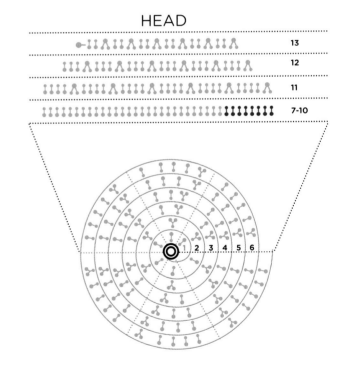

Ⓑ BODY

🔘 N 09 Gris Argent

ROUND	STITCHES	FORMULA
1	6	◎ 6 !
2	12	⅄ × 6
3	18	(⅄ + !) × 6
4	24	(⅄ + 2!) × 6
5-10	24	24 !
11	24	24 ! ●

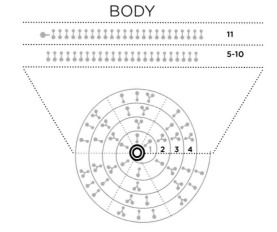

BODY

Ⓒ ARM X 2

🔘 N 09 Gris Argent
⚫ N 23 Passion

ROUND	STITCHES	FORMULA
1	6	◎ 6 !
2	9	(⅄ + !) × 3
3-4	9	9 !
5	9	9 !
6-9	9	9 !
10	9	9 ! ●

ARM

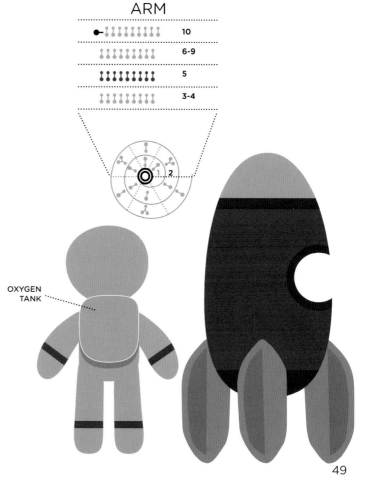

OXYGEN TANK

Ⓓ LEG X 2

⬤ N 09 Gris Argent

⬤ N 23 Passion

ROUND	STITCHES	FORMULA
1	6	◎ 6 ╏
2	12	Y × 6
3-4	12	12 ╏
5	12	12 ╏
6-10	12	12 ╏
11	12	12 ╏ ←

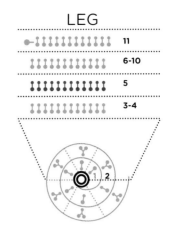

LEG

Ⓔ OXYGEN TANK

⬤ N 09 Gris Argent

ROUND	STITCHES	FORMULA
1	6	◎ 6 ╏
2	12	Y × 6
3	18	(Y + ╏) × 6
4-9	18	18 ╏
10	12	(Λ + ╏) × 6 ✿ Stuff
11	6	Λ × 6 ←

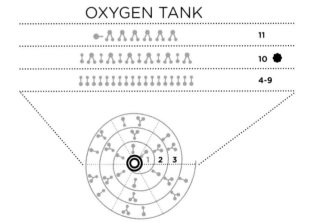

OXYGEN TANK

ASSEMBLING THE PARTS AND DETAILS

1. Crochet all the parts.

2. Stuff the head and the body. Then stuff the arms and legs with less stuffing towards the top edges.

3. Pin all the parts in position.

4. Sew the head onto the body. Then sew the arms and leg to the body.

5. Embroider the badge using N23 (Passion).

6. Sew the oxygen tank to the back of the figure as shown.

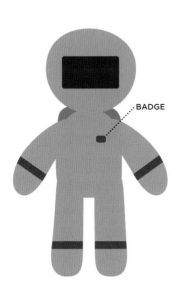

BADGE

ROCKET

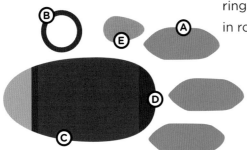

HOW TO CROCHET

Allways start with a magic ring of 6 stitches and work in rounds.

CHART SYMBOLS

- ◎ MAGIC RING
- ⬤ CHAIN STITCH
- 0 TURNING CHAIN
- ! DOUBLE CROCHET
- Y INCREASE
- Λ DECREASE
- ●━ SLIP STITCH

FIN

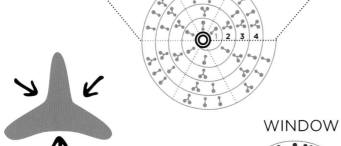

●━ΛΛΛΛΛΛ	17
!Λ!Λ!Λ!Λ!Λ!Λ	16
!!Λ!!Λ!!Λ!!Λ!!Λ	15
!!!!!!!!!!!!!!!!!!!!!!!!	5-14

Press each fin to this shape.

WINDOW

Ⓐ FIN X 3

N 64 Prussian

ROUND	STITCHES	FORMULA
1	6	◎ 6 !
2	12	Y × 6
3	18	(Y + !) × 6
4	24	(Y + 2 !) × 6
5-14	24	24 !
15	18	(Λ + 2 !) × 6
16	12	(Λ + !) × 6
17	6	Λ × 6 ●━

Ⓑ WINDOW

N 01 Ibiza

N 28 Zaphire

ROUND	STITCHES	FORMULA
1	6	◎ 6 !
2	12	Y × 6
3	18	(Y + !) × 6
4	24	(Y + 2 !) × 6 ●━

© BODY

- ⬤ N 09 Gris Argent
- ⬤ N 28 Zaphire
- ⬤ N 23 Passion

ROUND	STITCHES	FORMULA
1	6	◎ 6 !
2	12	Υ × 6
3	18	(Υ + !) × 6
4	18	18 !
5	24	(Υ + 2 !) × 6
6	24	24 !
7	30	(Υ + 3 !) × 6
8	30	30 !
9	36	(Υ + 4 !) × 6
10	36	36 !
11	42	(Υ + 5 !) × 6
12	42	42 !
13	48	(Υ + 6 !) × 6
14-29	48	48 !
30	42	(Λ + 6 !) × 6
31	36	(Λ + 5 !) × 6
32	30	(Λ + 4 !) × 6 ⬤

BODY

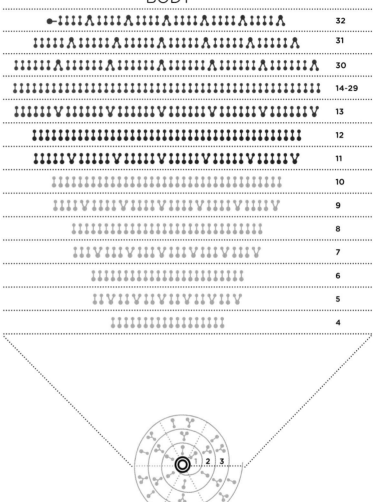

53

Ⓓ BOOSTER

● N 28 Zaphire

ROUND	STITCHES	FORMULA
1	6	◎ 6 !
2	12	Ⴤ × 6
3	18	(Ⴤ + !) × 6
4	24	(Ⴤ + 2 !) × 6
5	30	(Ⴤ + 3 !) × 6
6	30	30 !
7	30	30 ! ←

Ⓔ FLAMES

● N 47 Safran

ROUND	STITCHES	FORMULA
1	6	◎ 6 !
2	12	Ⴤ × 6
3	18	(Ⴤ + !) × 6
4	24	(Ⴤ + 2 !) × 6
5-6	24	24 !
7	18	(Λ + 2 !) × 6
8	18	18 !
9	12	(Λ + !) × 6 ✿ Stuff
10	12	12 !
11	6	Λ × 6 ←

BOOSTER

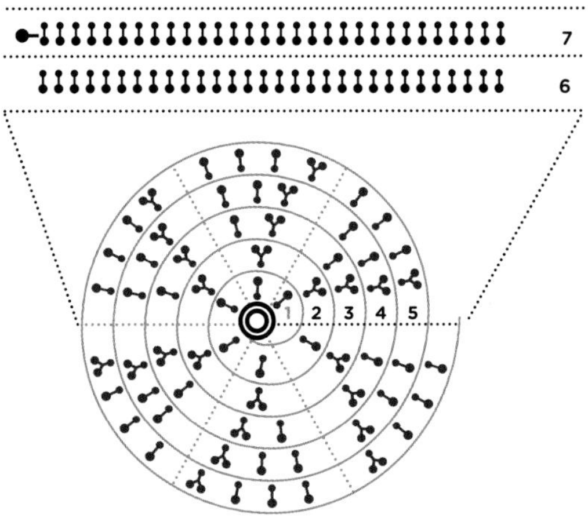

FLAMES

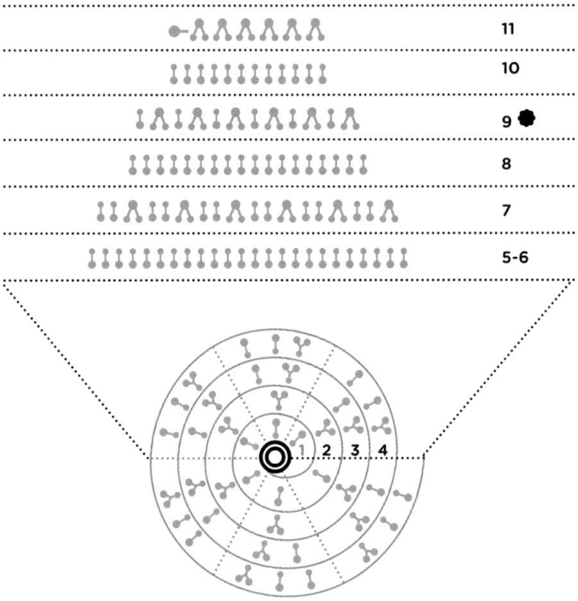

ASSEMBLING THE PARTS AND DETAILS

1. Crochet all the parts.

2. Stuff the rocket body, the booster and the flames. Close the flames once stuffed.

3. Press the fins into three parts and sew through all layers to hold folds in position.

4. Pin the parts in position.

5. Sew the window to the front of the rocket as shown.

6. Sew the booster to the base of the rocket body.

7. Sew the flames under the booster.

8. Sew the fins onto the rocket in positions as shown.

Finish the fins

3   Press them into three parts

3   Sew them using a sewing needle

2

4

DAVID
THE TINY AVIATOR

He flies his airplane to go and buy bread and milk for his breakfast.

YARNS:

DMC NATURA

- N 23   Passion
- N 75   Moss Green
- N 43   Golden Lemon
- N 27   Star Light
- N 01   Ibiza

MATERIALS:

· Stuffing
· 1 red button

TOOLS:

· 3 mm crochet hook
· Tapestry needle

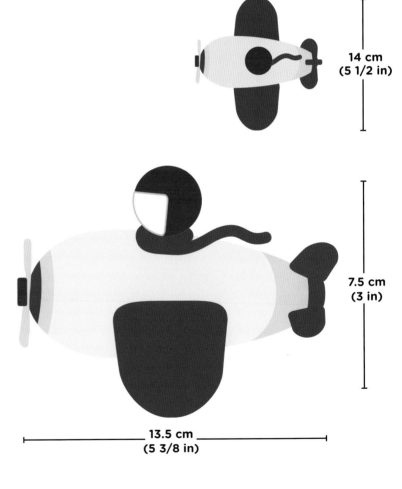

14 cm
(5 1/2 in)

7.5 cm
(3 in)

13.5 cm
(5 3/8 in)

DAVID

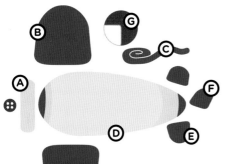

HOW TO CROCHET

Always start with a magic ring of 6 stitches. Work in rounds and finish all the parts of your amigurumi before stuffing them and adding details.

CHART SYMBOLS

◎ MAGIC RING
◠ CHAIN STITCH
0 TURNING CHAIN
↕ DOUBLE CROCHET
Y INCREASE
Λ DECREASE
●─ SLIP STITCH

PROPELLER

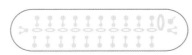

(A) PROPELLER

🟢 N 75 Moss Green

ROUND	STITCHES	FORMULA
1	10	◠ 10 0
2	10	10 ↕ + Y + 10 ↕ + Y ●─

WING

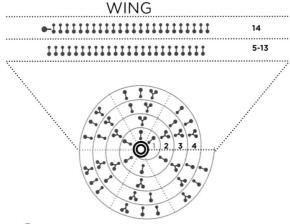

●─↕↕↕↕↕↕↕↕↕↕↕↕↕↕↕↕↕↕↕	14
↕↕↕↕↕↕↕↕↕↕↕↕↕↕↕↕↕↕↕↕↕↕↕↕	5-13

(B) WING X 2

🔴 N 27 Star Light

ROUND	STITCHES	FORMULA
1	6	◎ 6 ↕
2	12	Y × 6
3	18	(Y + ↕) × 6
4	24	(Y + 2↕) × 6
5-13	24	24 ↕
14	24	24 ↕ ●─

(C) SCARF

🔴 N 27 Star Light

ROUND	STITCHES	FORMULA
1	20	◠ 20 0
2	20	20 ↕ ●─

SCARF

●─↕↕↕↕↕↕↕↕↕↕↕↕↕↕↕↕↕↕↕↕↕	2
◠◠◠◠◠◠◠◠◠◠◠◠◠◠◠◠◠◠◠◠ 0	1

Ⓓ FUSELAGE

- ⬤ N 27 Star Light
- ◯ N 75 Moss Green
- ◯ N 43 Golden Lemon

ROUND	STITCHES	FORMULA
1	6	◎ 6 ⌡
2	12	Ƴ × 6
3	18	(Ƴ + ⌡) × 6
4	18	18 ⌡
5	24	(Ƴ + 2 ⌡) × 6
6	24	24 ⌡
7	30	(Ƴ + 3 ⌡) × 6
8	30	30 ⌡
9	36	(Ƴ + 4 ⌡) × 6
10	36	36 ⌡
11	42	(Ƴ + 5 ⌡) × 6
12-17	42	42 ⌡
18	36	(Λ + 5 ⌡) × 6
19-21	36	36 ⌡
22	30	(Λ + 4 ⌡) × 6
23-25	30	30 ⌡
26	24	(Λ + 3 ⌡) × 6
27-29	24	24 ⌡
30	18	(Λ + 2 ⌡) × 6
31-33	18	18 ⌡ ✿ Stuff
34	12	(Λ + ⌡) × 6
35	6	Λ × 6 ⊷

FUSELAGE

Ⓔ HORIZONTAL TAIL FIN X 2

⬤ N 27 Start Light

ROUND	STITCHES	FORMULA
1	6	◎ 6 ⑂
2	12	Ⓨ × 6
3-5	12	12 ⑂
6	12	12 ⑂ ←

HORIZONTAL TAIL FIN

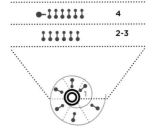

Ⓕ VERTICAL TAIL FIN

⬤ N 27 Start Light

ROUND	STITCHES	FORMULA
1	6	◎ 6 ⑂
2-3	6	6 ⑂
4	6	6 ⑂ ←

VERTICAL TAIL FIN

Ⓖ HEAD

⬤ N 23 Passion
◯ N 01 Ibiza

ROUND	STITCHES	FORMULA
1	6	◎ 6 ⑂
2	12	Ⓨ × 6
3	18	(Ⓨ + ⑂) × 6
4	24	(Ⓨ + 2 ⑂) × 6
5-6	24	6 ⑂ ◯ 18 ⑂ ⬤
7	18	(Λ + 2 ⑂) × 6
8	12	(Λ + ⑂) × 6 ←

HEAD

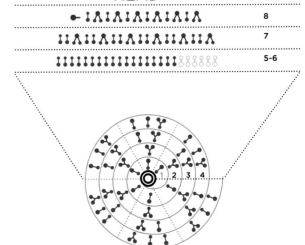

ASSEMBLING THE PARTS AND DETAILS

1. Crochet all the parts.

2. Close the fuselage once stuffed.

3. Do not stuff the wings, the vertical tail fin or the horizontal tail fins.

4. Press the wings flat and oversew the top edges. Do the same with the vertical and horizontal tail fins.

5. Pin all the parts in position.

6. Sew all the parts onto the fuselage as shown.

7. Sew the head onto the top of the plane.

8. Sew the red button to the centre of the propeller.

9. Sew the propeller to the front of the plane.

10. Wrap the scarf around the aviator's neck, then sew in place.

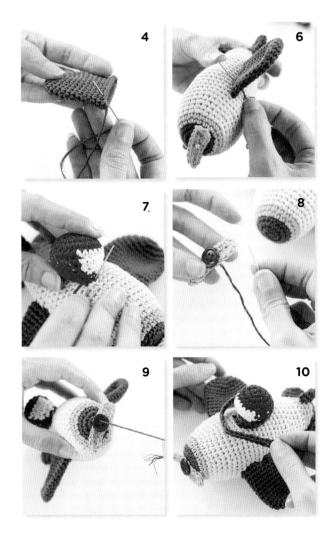

BETO
THE FISHING BOAT

You can sail around the world in this tiny fishing boat

YARNS:

DMC NATURA

- N 23   Passion
- N 22   Tropic Brown
- N 03   Sable
- N 26   Blue Jeans
- N 11   Noir

MATERIALS:

· Stuffing

TOOLS:

· 3 mm crochet hook
· Tapestry needle

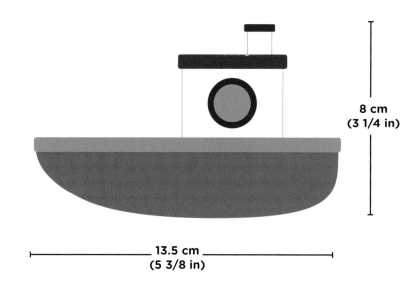

8 cm
(3 1/4 in)

13.5 cm
(5 3/8 in)

BETO

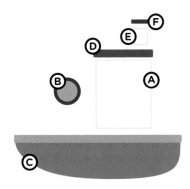

HOW TO CROCHET

Always start with a magic ring of 6 stitches. Work in rounds and finish all the parts of your amigurumi before stuffing them and adding the details.

CHART SYMBOLS

◎ MAGIC RING
● CHAIN STITCH
0 TURNING CHAIN
❢ DOUBLE CROCHET
Υ INCREASE
Λ DECREASE
●— SLIP STITCH

PILOTHOUSE

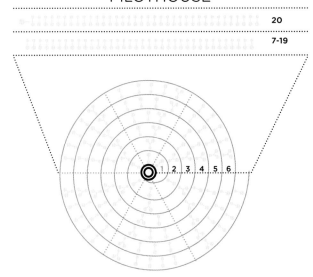

Ⓐ PILOTHOUSE

N 03 Sable

ROUND	STITCHES	FORMULA
1	6	◎ 6 ❢
2	12	Υ × 6
3	18	(Υ + ❢) × 6
4	24	(Υ + 2 ❢) × 6
5	30	(Υ + 3 ❢) × 6
6	36	(Υ + 4 ❢) × 6
7-19	36	❢ 36
20	36	❢ 36 ●—

WINDOW

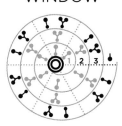

Ⓑ WINDOW X 2

N 26 Blue Jeans
N 11 Noir

ROUND	STITCHES	FORMULA
1	6	◎ 6 ❢
2	12	Υ × 6
3	18	(Υ + ❢) × 6 ●—

HULL

•‐ΛΛΛΛΛΛ	37
᛫Λ᛫Λ᛫Λ᛫Λ᛫Λ᛫Λ	36
᛫᛫Λ᛫᛫Λ᛫᛫Λ᛫᛫Λ᛫᛫Λ᛫᛫Λ	35
᛫᛫᛫Λ᛫᛫᛫Λ᛫᛫᛫Λ᛫᛫᛫Λ᛫᛫᛫Λ᛫᛫᛫Λ	34
᛫᛫᛫᛫Λ᛫᛫᛫᛫Λ᛫᛫᛫᛫Λ᛫᛫᛫᛫Λ᛫᛫᛫᛫Λ᛫᛫᛫᛫Λ	33
᛫᛫᛫᛫᛫Λ᛫᛫᛫᛫᛫Λ᛫᛫᛫᛫᛫Λ᛫᛫᛫᛫᛫Λ᛫᛫᛫᛫᛫Λ᛫᛫᛫᛫᛫Λ	32
᛫᛫	12-31
᛫᛫᛫᛫᛫V᛫᛫᛫᛫᛫V᛫᛫᛫᛫᛫V᛫᛫᛫᛫᛫V᛫᛫᛫᛫᛫V᛫᛫᛫᛫᛫V	11
᛫᛫᛫᛫᛫᛫᛫᛫᛫᛫᛫᛫᛫᛫᛫᛫᛫᛫᛫᛫᛫᛫᛫᛫᛫᛫᛫᛫᛫᛫᛫᛫᛫᛫᛫᛫	10
᛫᛫᛫᛫V᛫᛫᛫᛫V᛫᛫᛫᛫V᛫᛫᛫᛫V᛫᛫᛫᛫V᛫᛫᛫᛫V	9
᛫᛫᛫᛫᛫᛫᛫᛫᛫᛫᛫᛫᛫᛫᛫᛫᛫᛫᛫᛫᛫᛫᛫᛫᛫᛫᛫᛫᛫᛫	8
᛫᛫᛫V᛫᛫᛫V᛫᛫᛫V᛫᛫᛫V᛫᛫᛫V᛫᛫᛫V	7
᛫᛫᛫᛫᛫᛫᛫᛫᛫᛫᛫᛫᛫᛫᛫᛫᛫᛫᛫᛫᛫᛫᛫᛫	6
᛫᛫V᛫᛫V᛫᛫V᛫᛫V᛫᛫V᛫᛫V	5
᛫᛫᛫᛫᛫᛫᛫᛫᛫᛫᛫᛫᛫᛫᛫᛫᛫᛫	4

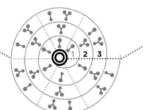

© HULL

⬤ N 22   Tropic Brown

ROUND	STITCHES	FORMULA
1	6	◎ 6 !
2	12	Υ × 6
3	18	(Υ + !) × 6
4	18	18 !
5	24	(Υ + 2 !) × 6
6	24	24 !
7	30	(Υ + 3 !) × 6
8	30	30 !
9	36	(Υ + 4 !) × 6
10	36	36 !
11	42	(Υ + 5 !) × 6
12-31	42	42 !
32	36	(Λ + 5 !) × 6
33	30	(Λ + 4 !) × 6
34	24	(Λ + 3 !) × 6
35	18	(Λ + 2 !) × 6
36	12	(Λ + !) × 6
37	6	Λ × 6 •‐

Ⓓ ROOF

⬤ N 23   Passion

ROUND	STITCHES	FORMULA
1	6	◎ 6 ❢
2	12	Υ × 6
3	18	(Υ + ❢) × 6
4	24	(Υ + 2❢) × 6
5	30	(Υ + 3❢) × 6
6	36	(Υ + 4❢) × 6
7	42	(Υ + 5❢) × 6 ←

ROOF

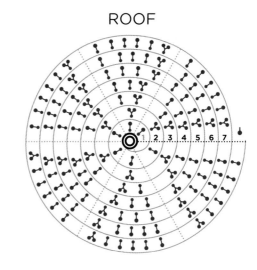

Ⓔ SMOKESTACK

⬤ N 03   Sable

ROUND	STITCHES	FORMULA
1	6	◎ 6 ❢
2	12	Υ × 6
3-7	12	❢ 12
8	12	❢ 12 ←

SMOKESTACK

Ⓕ SMOKESTACK TOP

⬤ N 11   Noir

ROUND	STITCHES	FORMULA
1	6	◎ 6 ❢
2	12	Υ × 6 ←

SMOKESTACK
TOP

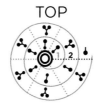

3

66

ASSEMBLING THE PARTS AND DETAILS

1. Crochet all the parts.

2. Stuff the pilothouse and the smokestack.

3. Press the hull together and oversew the top edges. Form into a boat shape, then, using N26 (Blue Jeans), work a round of double crochet all around the folded top edge.

4. Sew the roof to the top of the pilothouse.

5. Sew the smokestack top to the top of the smokestack.

6. Sew the bottom of the pilothouse inside the hull in position as shown.

7. Sew the smokestack to the pilothouse as shown.

8. Sew the windows to each side of the pilothouse.

9. Your finished fishing boat.

1-2

3

4

5

6

7

8

9

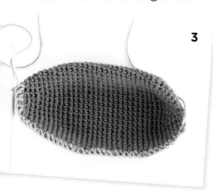

3

CURLY
AND HIS RACING CAR

Never again will you need gasoline to drive wherever you want.

YARNS:

DMC NATURA

- N 74 Curry
- N 64 Prussian
- N 09 Gris Argent
- N 11 Noir
- N 01 Ibiza

MATERIALS:

· Stuffing

TOOLS:

· 3 mm crochet hook
· Tapestry needle

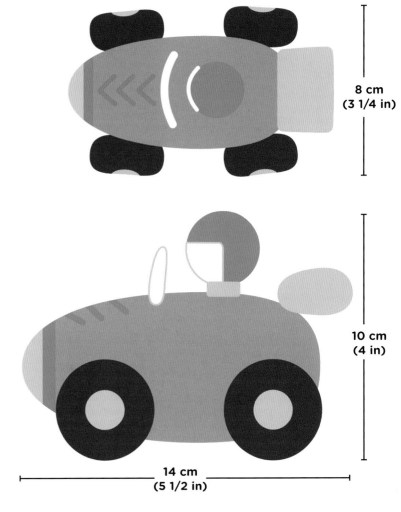

8 cm
(3 1/4 in)

10 cm
(4 in)

14 cm
(5 1/2 in)

CURLY

HOW TO CROCHET

Always start with a magic ring of 6 stitches. Work in rounds and finish all the parts of your amigurumi before stuffing them and adding the details.

CHART SYMBOLS

◎ MAGIC RING
➰ CHAIN STITCH
0 TURNING CHAIN
‡ DOUBLE CROCHET
Y INCREASE
Λ DECREASE
●➰ SLIP STITCH

Ⓐ
Ⓔ
Ⓑ
Ⓒ
Ⓓ SPOILER

Ⓐ HEAD

- N 64 Prussian
- N 01 Ibiza
- N 09 Gris Argent

ROUND	STITCHES	FORMULA
1	6	◎ 6 ‡
2	12	Y × 6
3	18	(Y + ‡) × 6
4	24	(Y + 2‡) × 6
5-6	24	6‡ ○ 18‡ ●
7	18	(Λ + 2‡) × 6
8	12	(Λ + ‡) × 6
9	12	12‡
10	12	12‡ ➰

HEAD

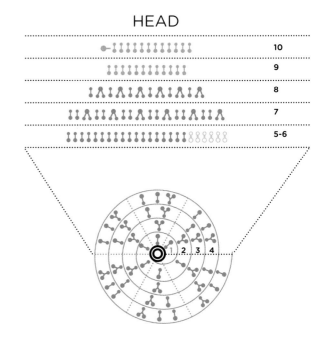

10
9
8
7
5-6

Ⓑ BODY

🔵 N 74 Curry
🔵 N 64 Prussian
🔵 N 09 Gris Argent

ROUND	STITCHES	FORMULA
1	6	◎ 6 ‼
2	12	Υ × 6
3	18	(Υ + ‼) × 6
4	18	18 ‼
5	24	(Υ + 2‼) × 6
6	24	24 ‼
7	30	(Υ + 3‼) × 6
8	30	30 ‼
9	36	(Υ + 4‼) × 6
10	36	36 ‼
11	42	(Υ + 5‼) × 6
12-31	42	42 ‼
32	36	(Λ + 5‼) × 6
33	30	(Λ + 4‼) × 6
34	24	(Λ + 3‼) × 6
35	18	(Λ + 2‼) × 6 ✿ Stuff
36	12	(Λ + ‼) × 6
37	6	Λ × 6 ⬅

BODY

Ⓒ WHEEL X 4

- 🔘 N 09 Gris Argent
- ⚫ N 11 Noir

ROUND	STITCHES	FORMULA
1	6	◎ 6 !
2	12	Y × 6
3	18	(Y + !) × 6
4	24	(Y + 2 !) × 6
5	30	(Y + 3 !) × 6
6	30	30 !
7	24	(Λ + 3 !) × 6
8	18	(Λ + 2 !) × 6 ✿ Stuff
9	12	(Λ + !) × 6
10	6	Λ × 6 ←

Ⓓ SPOILER

- 🔘 N 09 Gris Argent

ROUND	STITCHES	FORMULA
1	6	◎ 6 !
2	12	Y × 6
3-11	12	12 !
12	6	Λ × 6 ←

Ⓔ WINDSHIELD

- ⚪ N 01 Ibiza

ROUND	STITCHES	FORMULA
1	6	◎ 6 !
2-11	6	6 !
12	6	6 ! ←

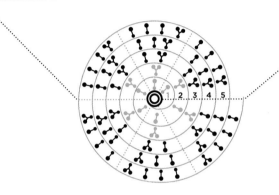

WHEEL

● ‑ Λ Λ Λ Λ Λ	10
! Λ ! Λ ! Λ ! Λ ! Λ	9
! ! Λ ! ! Λ ! ! Λ ! ! Λ ! ! Λ ! ! Λ	8 ✿
! ! ! Λ ! ! ! Λ ! ! ! Λ ! ! ! Λ ! ! ! Λ ! ! ! Λ	7
! !	6

SPOILER

● ‑ Λ Λ Λ Λ Λ Λ	12
! ! ! ! ! ! ! ! ! ! ! !	3-11

WINDSHIELD

⚬‑ 8 8 8 8 8 8	12
8 8 8 8 8 8	2-11

ASSEMBLING THE PARTS AND DETAILS

1. Crochet all the parts.

2. Close the car body once stuffed.

3. Using N64 (Prussian) embroider the stitches on the car body following the stitch diagram and photo.

4. Stuff the other parts except the windshield.

5. Press the windshield flat and oversew the edges.

6. Pin the parts in position.

7. Sew the four wheels to the car body in positions as shown.

8. Sew the head, the spoiler and the windshield onto the car as shown.

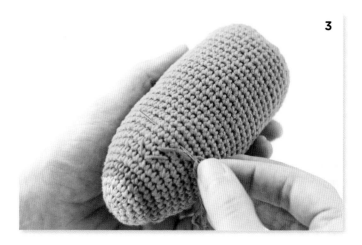

Stitch diagram

LUCY & BOBBY
TWO CUTE KIDS

They have style, they have charm and they are the latin lovers of the Kindergarten.

YARNS FOR LUCY:

DMC NATURA
- N 01 Ibiza
- N 36 Gardenia
- N 22 Tropic Brown
- N 61 Crimson
- N 43 Golden Lemon
- N 14 Green Valley
- N 11 Noir

YARNS FOR BOBBY:

DMC NATURA
- N 36 Gardenia
- N 28 Zaphire
- N 22 Tropic Brown
- N 49 Turquoise
- N 75 Moss Green
- N 11 Noir

MATERIALS:
- 1 Pair of transparent safety eyes 10mm
- Stuffing

TOOLS:
- 3 mm crochet hook
- Tapestry needle

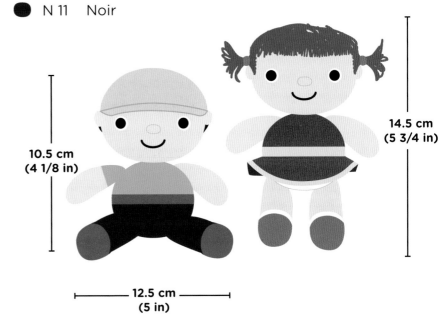

10.5 cm (4 1/8 in)

14.5 cm (5 3/4 in)

12.5 cm (5 in)

LUCY

HOW TO CROCHET

Always start with a magic ring of 6 stitches. Work in rounds and finish all the parts of your amigurumi before stuffing them and adding the face details.

CHART SYMBOLS

- ◎ MAGIC RING
- ⌒ CHAIN STITCH
- 0 TURNING CHAIN
- ⚡ DOUBLE CROCHET
- ⋎ INCREASE
- ⋏ DECREASE
- ● SLIP STITCH

Ⓐ HEAD

N 36 Gardenia

ROUND	STITCHES	FORMULA
1	6	◎ 6 ⚡
2	12	⋎ x 6
3	18	(⋎ + ⚡) x 6
4	24	(⋎ + 2 ⚡) x 6
5	30	(⋎ + 3 ⚡) x 6
6	36	(⋎ + 4 ⚡) x 6
7	42	(⋎ + 5 ⚡) x 6
8	48	(⋎ + 6 ⚡) x 6
9	54	(⋎ + 7 ⚡) x 6
10	60	(⋎ + 8 ⚡) x 6
11-16	60	⚡ 60
17	54	(⋏ + 8 ⚡) x 6
18	48	(⋏ + 7 ⚡) x 6
19	42	(⋏ + 6 ⚡) x 6
20	36	(⋏ + 5 ⚡) x 6
21	30	(⋏ + 4 ⚡) x 6
22	24	(⋏ + 3 ⚡) x 6 ●

HEAD

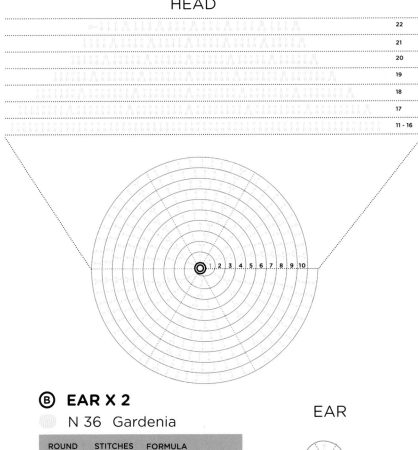

Ⓑ EAR X 2

N 36 Gardenia

ROUND	STITCHES	FORMULA
1	6	◎ 6 ⚡ ●

EAR

© BODY

○ N 01 Ibiza
● N 61 Crimson
○ N 43 Golden Lemon

ROUND	STITCHES	FORMULA
1	6	◎ 6 !
2	12	Y × 6
3	18	(Y + !) × 6
4	24	(Y + 2 !) × 6
5	30	(Y + 3 !) × 6
6	36	(Y + 4 !) × 6
7	42	(Y + 5 !) × 6
8-9	42	! 42
10-11	42	! 42
12-14	42	! 42
15	36	(Λ + 5 !) × 6
16	30	(Λ + 4 !) × 6
17	24	(Λ + 3 !) × 6 ←

BODY

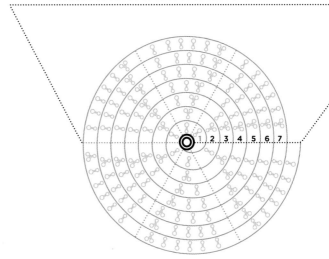

ⓓ ARM X 2

○ N 36 Gardenia

ROUND	STITCHES	FORMULA
1	6	◎ 6 !
2	12	Y × 6
3-11	12	12 !
12	12	12 ! ←

ARM

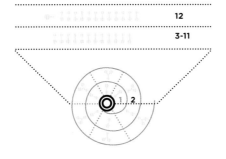

Ⓔ LEG X 2

- 🟢 N 14 Green Valley
- ⚪ N 01 Ibiza
- ⚪ N 36 Gardenia

ROUND	STITCHES	FORMULA
1	6	◎ 6 !
2	12	Y × 6
3	18	(Y + !) × 6
4	24	(Y + 2 !) × 6
5	24	24 !
6	18	(⅄ + 2 !) × 6
7-8	18	18 !
9-13	18	18 !
14	18	18 !•−

LEG

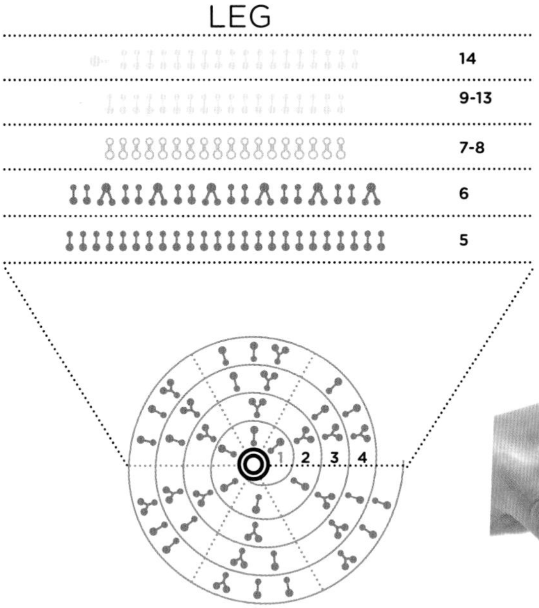

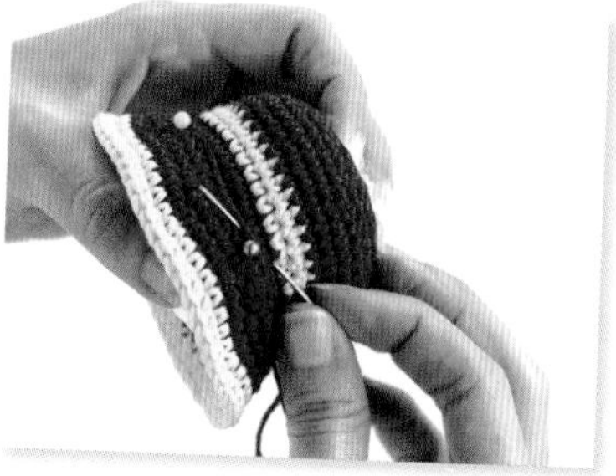

Ⓕ SKIRT

- ⚫ N 61 Crimson
- ⚪ N 43 Golden Lemon

Start by making a chain of 42 stitches

ROUND	STITCHES	FORMULA
1	42	○ 42 •−
2	42	! 42
3	48	(Y + 6 !) × 6
4	48	! 48
5	54	(Y + 7 !) × 6
6	54	! 54 •−

SKIRT

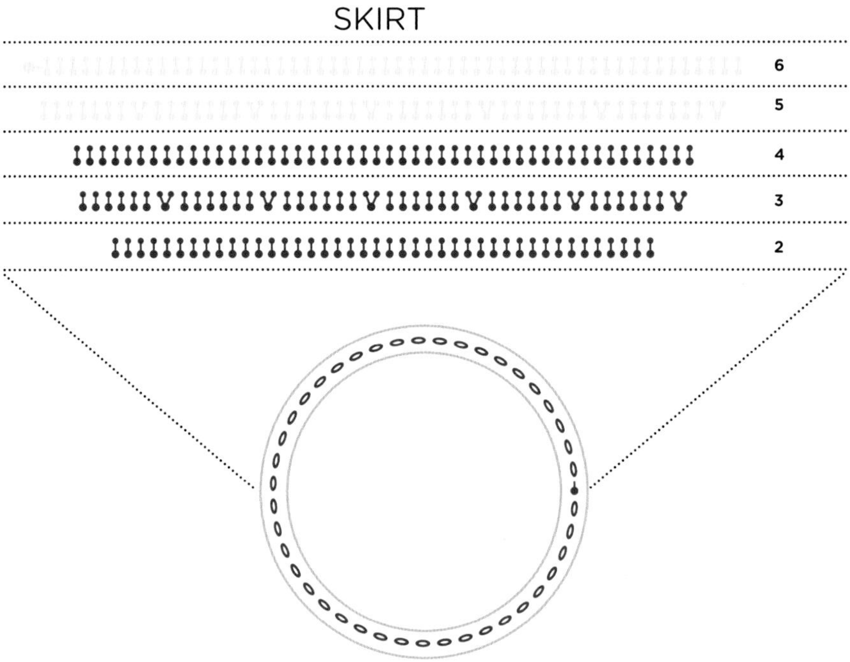

ASSEMBLING THE PARTS AND DETAILS

1. Crochet all the parts.

2. Stuff the head and the body. Then stuff the arms and legs with less stuffing towards the top edges.

3. Attach the safety eyes and sew on the ears. Embroider the nose using N36 (Gardenia) and the mouth using N11 (Noir).

4. Thread a length of N22 (Tropic Brown) onto a needle and knot one end. Insert the needle into the head in front of one ear and bring it out at the centre top.

5. Sew lines over and around the head outwards from the centre.

6. Repeat step 5 until all of the head is covered.

7. Then thread the needle with more yarn, knotted at one end, and push the needle through the bottom of the head and out at the sides where the bunches are going to be.

8. Snip off the excess yarn. Repeat the process several times until you have a bunch of 'hair'.

9. Using N14 (Green Valley) wrap around the bunch, close to the head and then sew underneath to secure.

10. Trim the hair to an even length.

11. Sew the top edge of the skirt to the body.

12. Sew the head onto the body. Then sew on the arms and legs.

BOBBY

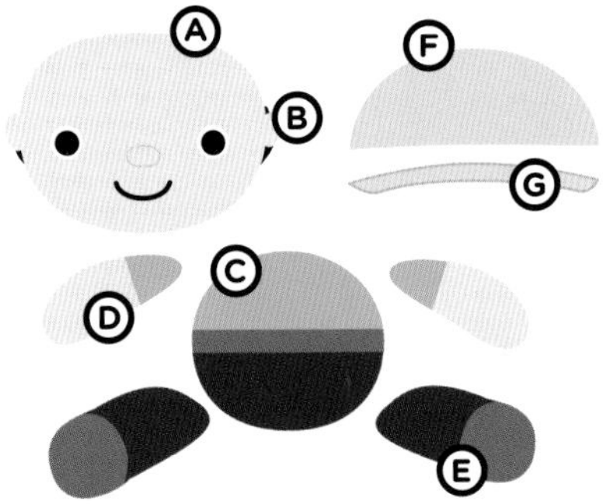

HOW TO CROCHET

Always start with a magic ring of 6 stitches. Work in rounds and finish all the parts of your amigurumi before stuffing them and adding the face details.

CHART SYMBOLS

◎ MAGIC RING
⬭ CHAIN STITCH
0 TURNING CHAIN
I DOUBLE CROCHET
Y INCREASE
Λ DECREASE
●- SLIP STITCH

Ⓐ HEAD

N 36 Gardenia

ROUND	STITCHES	FORMULA
1	6	◎ 6 I
2	12	Y x 6
3	18	(Y + I) x 6
4	24	(Y + 2 I) x 6
5	30	(Y + 3 I) x 6
6	36	(Y + 4 I) x 6
7	42	(Y + 5 I) x 6
8	48	(Y + 6 I) x 6
9	54	(Y + 7 I) x 6
10	60	(Y + 8 I) x 6
11-16	60	I 60
17	54	(Λ + 8 I) x 6
18	48	(Λ + 7 I) x 6
19	42	(Λ + 6 I) x 6
20	36	(Λ + 5 I) x 6
21	30	(Λ + 4 I) x 6
22	24	(Λ + 3 I) x 6 ●-

HEAD

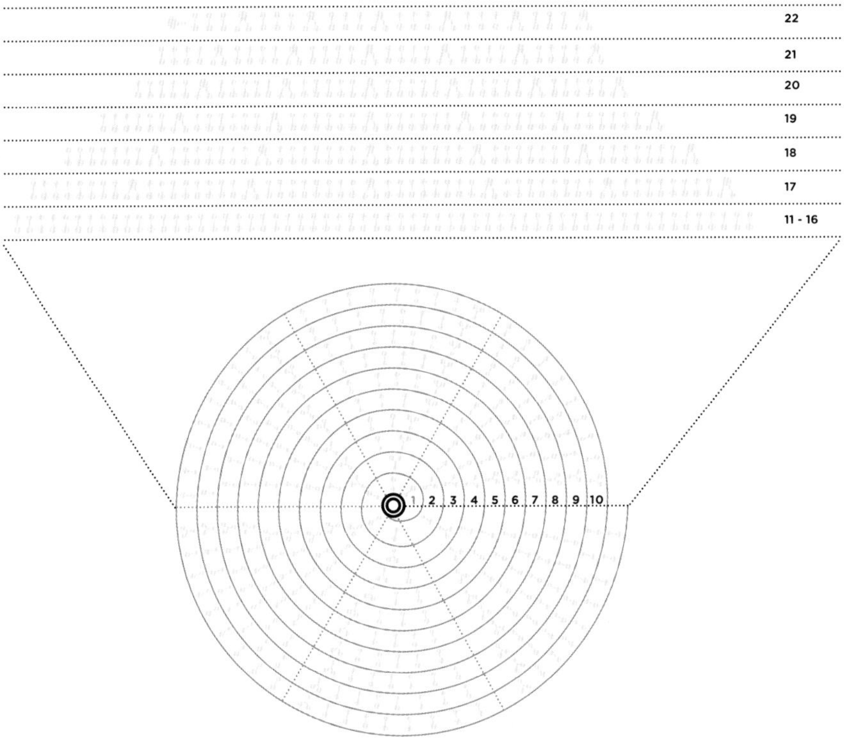

Ⓑ EAR X 2

N 36 Gardenia

ROUND	STITCHES	FORMULA
1	6	◎ 6 I ●-

EAR

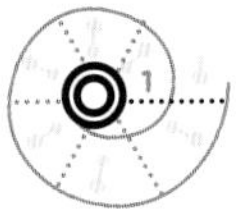

Ⓒ BODY

- ⬤ N 28 Zaphire
- ⬤ N 22 Tropic Brown
- ⬤ N 49 Turquoise

ROUND	STITCHES	FORMULA
1	6	◎ 6 !
2	12	Υ × 6
3	18	(Υ + !) × 6
4	24	(Υ + 2 !) × 6
5	30	(Υ + 3 !) × 6
6	36	(Υ + 4 !) × 6
7	42	(Υ + 5 !) × 6
8-9	42	! 42
10	42	! 42
11-14	42	! 42
15	36	(Λ + 5 !) × 6
16	30	(Λ + 4 !) × 6
17	24	(Λ + 3 !) × 6 •

BODY

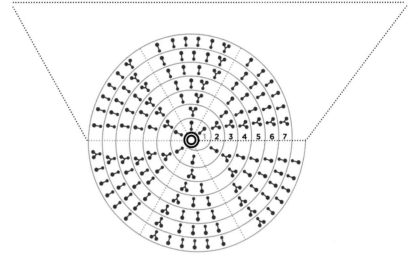

Ⓓ ARM X 2

- ⬤ N 36 Gardenia
- ⬤ N 49 Turquoise

ROUND	STITCHES	FORMULA
1	6	◎ 6 !
2	12	Υ × 6
3-8	12	12 !
9-11	12	12 !
12	12	12 ! •

ARM

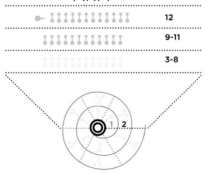

Ⓔ LEG X 2

● N 28 Zaphire
● N 22 Tropic Brown

ROUND	STITCHES	FORMULA
1	6	◎ 6 !
2	12	Υ × 6
3	18	(Υ + !) × 6
4	24	(Υ + 2 !) × 6
5	24	24 !
6	18	(Λ + 2 !) × 6
7-13	18	18 !
14	18	18 ! ●

Ⓕ CAP

● N 75 Moss Green

ROUND	STITCHES	FORMULA
1	6	◎ 6 !
2	12	Υ × 6
3	18	(Υ + !) × 6
4	24	(Υ + 2 !) × 6
5	30	(Υ + 3 !) × 6
6	36	(Υ + 4 !) × 6
7	42	(Υ + 5 !) × 6
8	48	(Υ + 6 !) × 6
9	54	(Υ + 7 !) × 6
10	60	(Υ + 8 !) × 6
11	66	(Υ + 9 !) × 6
12	66	! 66
13	66	! 66 ●

LEG

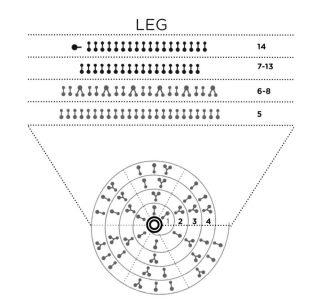

CAP

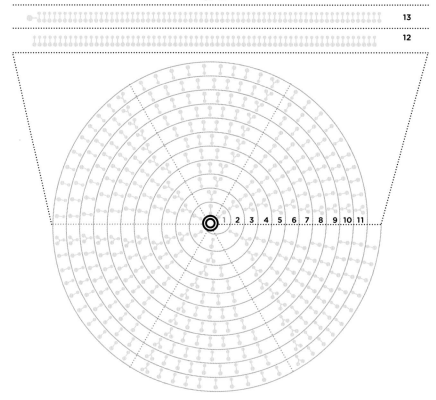

ASSEMBLING THE PARTS AND DETAILS

1. Crochet all the parts.

2. Stuff the head and the body. Then stuff the arms and legs with less stuffing towards the top edges.

3. Attach the safety eyes, embroider the nose using N36 (Gardenia) and then sew on the ears.

4. Embroider the mouth using N11 (Noir).

5. Thread a length of N11 (Noir) onto a needle and knot the end.

6. Push the needle through the bottom of the head and out behind the ears. Sew straight lines all around the back of the head level with the ears.

7. Repeat until you reach the other ear.

8. Sew the edge of the cap peak to the cap, then sew the cap to the doll's head.

9. Sew the head onto the body. Then sew on the arms and legs.

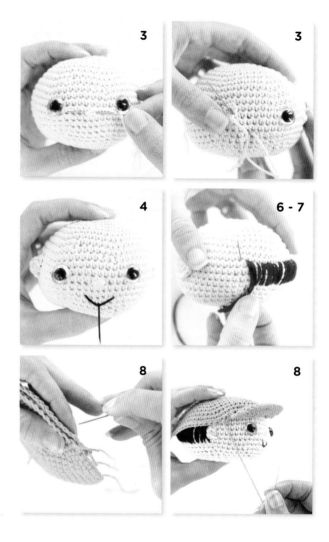

Ⓖ CAP PEAK

N 75 Moss Green

ROUND	STITCHES	FORMULA
1	20	⌐ 20 ◊
2	20	20 ◊◊
3	20	20 ◊←

CAP PEAK

THREE TINY BIRDS
TWEET, TWEET, TWEET

They come from far away to tell you all the gossip!

YARNS:

DMC NATURA

- N 47   Safran
- N 30   Glicine
- N 13   Pistache
- N 13   Tournesol
- N 11   Noir

MATERIALS:

· Stuffing
· 2/3 pair of safety eyes 6mm

TOOLS:

· 3 mm crochet hook
· Tapestry needle

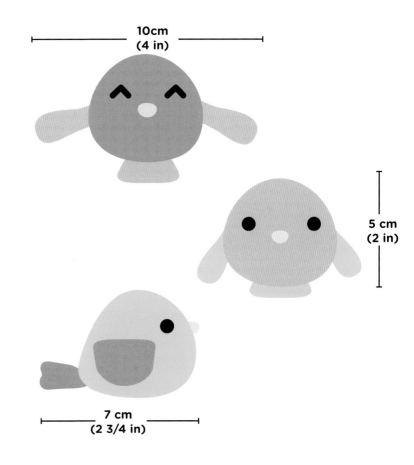

10cm
(4 in)

5 cm
(2 in)

7 cm
(2 3/4 in)

TINY BIRDS

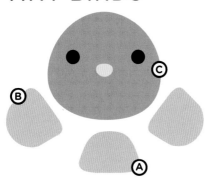

HOW TO CROCHET

Always start with a magic ring of 6 stitches. Work in rounds and finish all the parts of your amigurumi before stuffing them and adding the face details.

CHART SYMBOLS

- ◎ MAGIC RING
- ➊ CHAIN STITCH
- ᛁ TURNING CHAIN
- ᛁ DOUBLE CROCHET
- Ⲩ INCREASE
- Ⲁ DECREASE
- ➊ SLIP STITCH

Ⓐ TAIL

N 30 Glicine

ROUND	STITCHES	FORMULA
1	6	◎ 6 ᛁ
2	12	Ⲩ × 6
3	18	(Ⲩ + ᛁ) × 6
4	18	18 ᛁ
5	18	18 ᛁ ➊

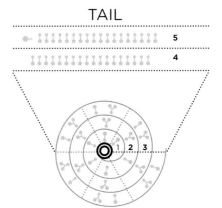

TAIL

Ⓑ WING X 2

N 30 Glicine

ROUND	STITCHES	FORMULA
1	6	◎ 6 ᛁ
2	12	Ⲩ × 6
3-6	12	12 ᛁ
7	12	12 ᛁ ➊

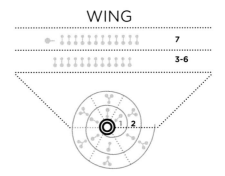

WING

© BODY

N 47 Safran

ROUND	STITCHES	FORMULA
1	6	◎ 6 !
2	12	Y × 6
3	18	(Y + !) × 6
4	18	18 !
5	24	(Y + 2 !) × 6
6	24	24 !
7	30	(Y + 3 !) × 6
8	30	30 !
9	36	(Y + 4 !) × 6
10	36	36 !
11	42	(Y + 5 !) × 6
12	42	42 !
13	36	(Λ + 5 !) × 6
14	30	(Λ + 4 !) × 6
15	24	(Λ + 3 !) × 6
16	18	(Λ + 2 !) × 6 ❀ Stuff
17	12	(Λ + !) × 6
18	6	Λ × 6 ←

BODY

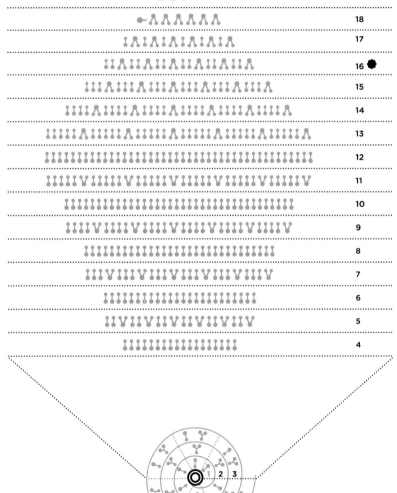

COLOUR COMBINATIONS

With this same pattern you can make all three birds, just change the colours as the suggestions here or pick your own.

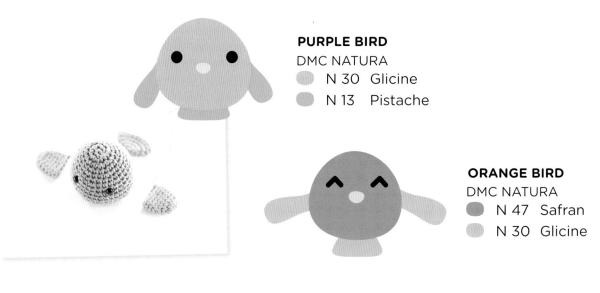

PURPLE BIRD
DMC NATURA

- N 30 Glicine
- N 13 Pistache

ORANGE BIRD
DMC NATURA

- N 47 Safran
- N 30 Glicine

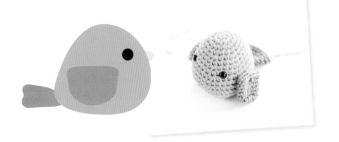

GREEN BIRD
DMC NATURA

- N 13 Pistache
- N 47 Safran

ASSEMBLING THE PARTS AND DETAILS

1. Crochet all the parts.

2. If you are using safety eyes, attach them.

3. Close the body once stuffed.

4. Oversew the edges of the wings and tail then sew them to the body.

5. Embroider the eyes using N11 (Noir) and the beak using N13 (Tournesol) as shown.

6. Now they are ready for flying!

3

4

5

5

6

LILY & BILLY
TWO LUCKY FISH

Mother and son, swimming around the reef looking for lucky coins.

YARNS:

DMC NATURA

- N 76 Lima
- N 23 Passion
- N 44 Prussian
- N 11 Noir

MATERIALS:

· 1 Pair of black safety eyes 6mm
· 1 Pair of black safety eyes 4,5 mm
· Stuffing

TOOLS:

· 3 mm crochet hook
· Tapestry needle

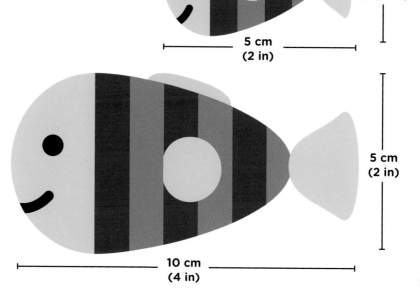

3 cm
(1 1/4 in)

5 cm
(2 in)

5 cm
(2 in)

10 cm
(4 in)

LILY

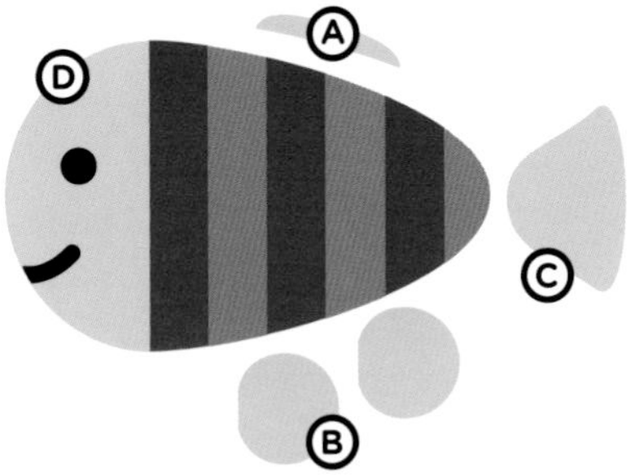

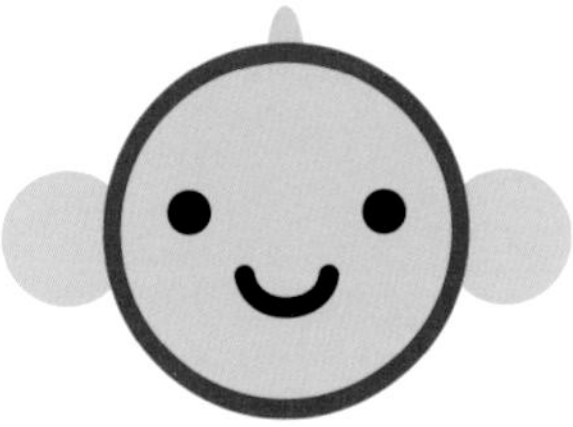

HOW TO CROCHET

Always start with a magic ring of 6 stitches. Work in rounds and finish all the parts of your amigurumi before stuffing them and adding the face details.

CHART SYMBOLS

◎ MAGIC RING
⬭ CHAIN STITCH
0 TURNING CHAIN
I DOUBLE CROCHET
Y INCREASE
Λ DECREASE
●– SLIP STITCH

Ⓐ DORSAL FIN

N 76 Lima

ROW	STITCHES	FORMULA
1	5	⬭ 5 0
2	5	5 I ●–

DORSAL FIN

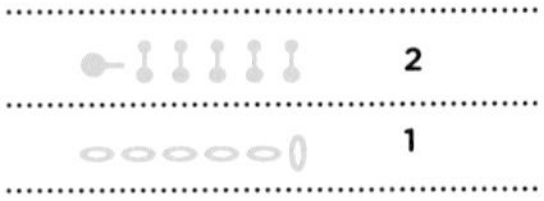

Ⓑ FIN X 2

N 76 Lima

ROUND	STITCHES	FORMULA
1	6	◎ 6 I
2	12	Y x 6 ●–

FIN

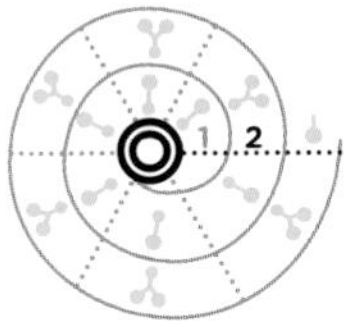

Ⓒ TAIL

N 76 Lima

ROUND	STITCHES	FORMULA
1	6	◎ 6 I
2	12	Y x 6
3	12	12 I
4	18	(Y + I) x 6
5	24	(Y + 2 I) x 6 ●–

TAIL

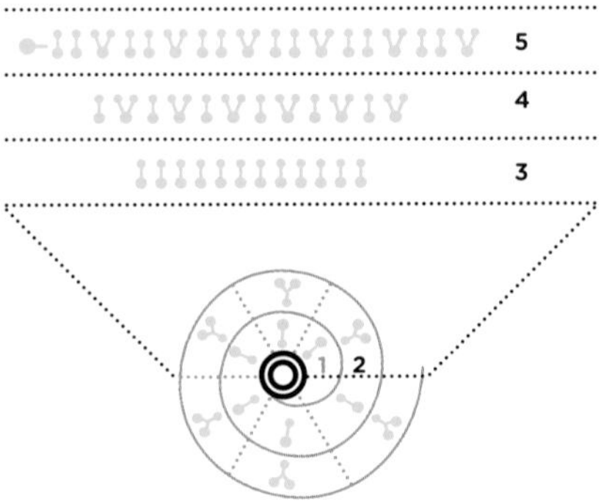

Ⓓ BODY

- N 76 Lima
- N 23 Passion
- N 64 Prussian

ROUND	STITCHES	FORMULA
1	6	◎ 6 !
2	12	⅄ × 6
3	18	(⅄ + !) × 6
4	24	(⅄ + 2 !) × 6
5	30	(⅄ + 3 !) × 6
6	36	(⅄ + 4 !) × 6
7	42	(⅄ + 5 !) × 6
8-10	42	42 !
11	36	(⋏ + 5 !) × 6
12-13	36	36 !
14	30	(⋏ + 4 !) × 6
15-16	30	30 !
17	24	(⋏ + 3 !) × 6
18-19	24	24 !
20	18	(⋏ + 2 !) × 6
21-22	18	18 ! ❁ Stuff
23	12	(⋏ + !) × 6
24-25	12	12 !
26	6	⋏ × 6 ⊶

BODY

BILLY

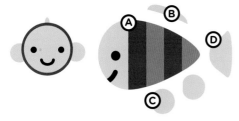

FINS

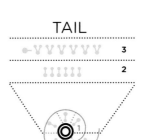

TAIL

3

2

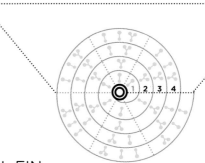

Ⓒ FIN X 2

N 76 Lima

ROUND	STITCHES	FORMULA
1	6	◎ 6 ! ←

Ⓓ TAIL

N 76 Lima

ROUND	STITCHES	FORMULA
1	6	◎ 6 !
2	6	6 !
3	12	Y × 6 ←

Ⓐ BODY

N 76 Lima
N 23 Passion
N 64 Prussian

ROUND	STITCHES	FORMULA
1	6	◎ 6 !
2	12	Y × 6
3	18	(Y + !) × 6
4	24	(Y + 2 !) × 6
5-6	24	24 !
7	18	(Λ + 2 !) × 6
8	18	18 ! ✿ Stuff
9	12	(Λ + !) × 6
10	12	12 !
11	6	Λ × 6 ←

BODY

11

10

9

8 ✿

7

5-6

Ⓑ DORSAL FIN

N 76 Lima

ROW	STITCHES	FORMULA
1	4	⌒ 4 0
2	4	4 ! ←

DORSAL FIN

2

1

94

ASSEMBLING THE PARTS AND DETAILS

1. Before finishing the body, attach the safety eyes and embroider the mouth.

2. Stuff and close the body.

3. Sew the fins 'to the body level with the eyes.

4. Sew the dorsal fin to the body. Then sew the tail in position.

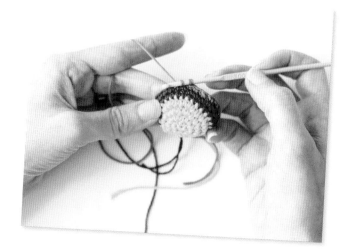

DEE-DEE
THE POLITE PUPPY

She is very polite and always so excited to see you.

YARNS:

DMC NATURA

- N 37   Canelle
- N 22   Tropic Brown
- N 23   Passion
- N 11   Noir

MATERIALS:

· Stuffing
· 1 Pair of black safety eyes 6mm
· 1 Brown plastic nose

TOOLS:

· 3 mm crochet hook
· Tapestry needle

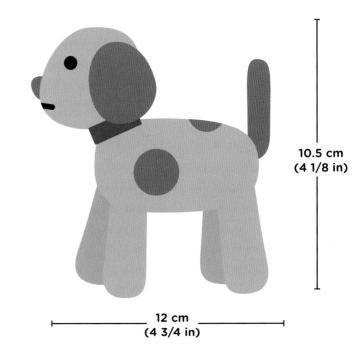

10.5 cm
(4 1/8 in)

12 cm
(4 3/4 in)

DEE-DEE

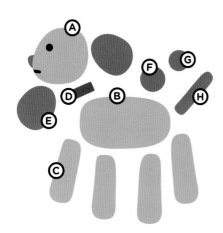

HOW TO CROCHET

Always start with a magic ring of 6 stitches. Work in rounds and finish all the parts of your amigurumi before stuffing them and adding the face details.

CHART SYMBOLS

◎ MAGIC RING
� CHAIN STITCH
0 TURNING CHAIN
❗ DOUBLE CROCHET
Y INCREASE
Λ DECREASE
●— SLIP STITCH

Ⓐ HEAD

N 37   Canelle

ROUND	STITCHES	FORMULA
1	6	◎ 6 ❗
2	12	Y × 6
3	18	(Y + ❗) × 6
4-5	18	❗ 18
6	24	(Y + 2❗) × 6
7	30	(Y + 3❗) × 6
8	36	(Y + 4❗) × 6
9-10	36	❗ 36
11	30	(Λ + 4❗) × 6
12	24	(Λ + 3❗) × 6
13	18	(Λ + 2❗) × 6 ● Stuff
14	12	(Λ + ❗) × 6
15	6	Λ + × 6 ●—

HEAD

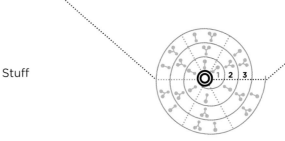

●—ΛΛΛΛΛΛ	15
❗Λ❗Λ❗Λ❗Λ❗Λ❗Λ	14
❗❗Λ❗❗Λ❗❗Λ❗❗Λ❗❗Λ❗❗Λ	13 ●
❗❗❗Λ❗❗❗Λ❗❗❗Λ❗❗❗Λ❗❗❗Λ❗❗❗Λ	12
❗❗❗❗Λ❗❗❗❗Λ❗❗❗❗Λ❗❗❗❗Λ❗❗❗❗Λ❗❗❗❗Λ	11
❗❗❗❗❗❗❗❗❗❗❗❗❗❗❗❗❗❗❗❗❗❗❗❗❗❗❗❗❗❗❗❗❗❗❗❗	9-10
❗❗❗❗Y❗❗❗❗Y❗❗❗❗Y❗❗❗❗Y❗❗❗❗Y❗❗❗❗Y	8
❗❗❗Y❗❗❗Y❗❗❗Y❗❗❗Y❗❗❗Y❗❗❗Y	7
❗❗Y❗❗Y❗❗Y❗❗Y❗❗Y❗❗Y	6
❗❗❗❗❗❗❗❗❗❗❗❗❗❗❗❗❗❗	4-5

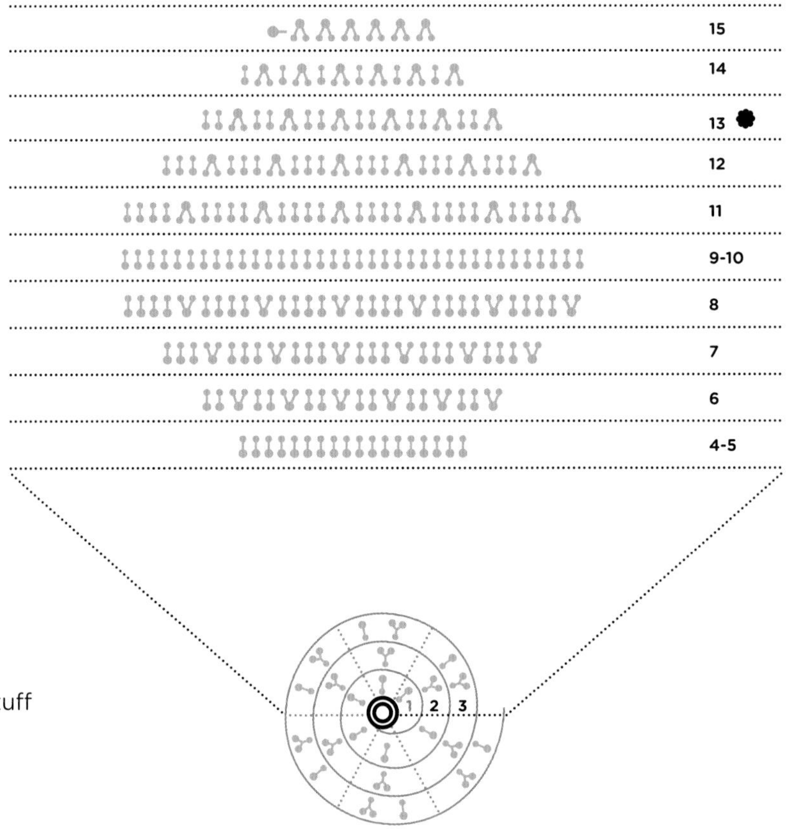

Ⓑ BODY

🔘 N 37 Canelle

ROUND	STITCHES	FORMULA
1	6	◎ 6 !
2	12	Ƴ × 6
3	18	(Ƴ + !) × 6
4	24	(Ƴ + 2 !) × 6
5	30	(Ƴ + 3 !) × 6
6-9	30	! 30
10	24	(Λ + 3 !) × 6
11-18	24	! 24
19	18	(Λ + 2 !) × 6 ✿ Stuff
20	12	(Λ + !) × 6
21	6	Λ × 6 •—

Ⓒ LEG X 4

🔘 N 37 Canelle

ROUND	STITCHES	FORMULA
1	6	◎ 6 !
2	12	Ƴ × 6
3-11	12	12 !
12	12	12 ! •—

Ⓓ COLLAR

⬤ N 23 Passion

ROW	STITCHES	FORMULA
1	20	◠ 20 ◖
2	20	20 ! •—

BODY

•— Λ Λ Λ Λ Λ	21
! Λ ! Λ ! Λ ! Λ ! Λ	20
! ! Λ ! ! Λ ! ! Λ ! ! Λ ! ! Λ ! ! Λ	19 ✿
! !	11-18
! ! ! Λ ! ! ! Λ ! ! ! Λ ! ! ! Λ ! ! ! Λ ! ! ! Λ	10
! !	6-9

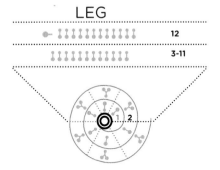

LEG

•— ! ! ! ! ! ! ! ! ! ! ! !	12
! ! ! ! ! ! ! ! ! ! ! !	3-11

COLLAR

•— !	2
◦ ◖	1

Ⓔ EAR X 2

● N 22 Tropic Brown

ROUND	STITCHES	FORMULA
1	6	◎ 6 ⌡
2	12	Ⴘ × 6
3-8	12	12 ⌡
9	6	Λ × 6 ●

EAR

Ⓕ BIG SPOT

● N 22 Tropic Brown

ROUND	STITCHES	FORMULA
1	6	◎ 6 ⌡
2	12	Ⴘ × 6 ●

BIG SPOT

Ⓖ LITTLE SPOT

● N 22 Tropic Brown

ROUND	STITCHES	FORMULA
1	6	◎ 6 ⌡ ●

LITTLE SPOT

Ⓗ TAIL

● N 22 Tropic Brown

ROUND	STITCHES	FORMULA
1	6	◎ 6 ⌡
2-8	6	6 ⌡
9	6	6 ⌡ ●

TAIL

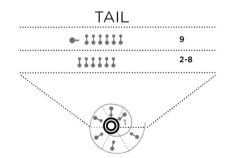

ASSEMBLING THE PARTS AND DETAILS

1. Once you have finished all the parts, stuff them. Do not stuff the ears and the tail.

2. Attach the safety eyes and nose then close the head.

3. Press the ears flat then oversew the top edges.

4. Embroider the mouth using N 11 (Noir).

5. Pin all the parts position.

6. Sew the legs onto the body. Then, sew on the spots.

7. Sew the head onto the body.

8. Sew the tail onto the back of the body.

9. Finally, wrap the collar around the neck then sew in place to secure.

2

4

5

7

YOYO
THE KNITTING CAT

Give him a ball of yarn and he will knit you a sweater.

YARNS:

DMC NATURA

	N 35	Nacar
	N 16	Tournesol
	N 14	Green Valley
	N 11	Noir
	N 44	Agatha

MATERIALS:

· Stuffing
· 1 Pair of safety eyes 9mm

TOOLS:

· 3 mm crochet hook
· Tapestry needle

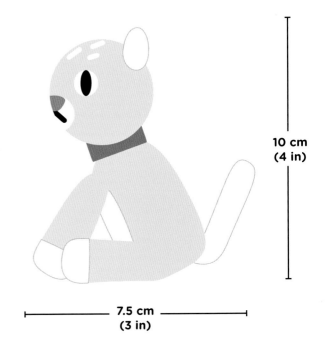

10 cm
(4 in)

7.5 cm
(3 in)

YOYO

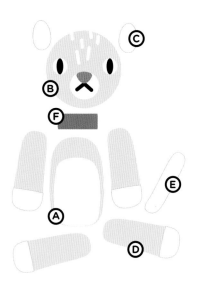

HOW TO CROCHET

Always start with a magic ring of 6 stitches. Work in rounds and finish all the parts of your amigurumi before stuffing them and adding the face details.

CHART SYMBOLS

- ◎ MAGIC RING
- ● CHAIN STITCH
- ◖ TURNING CHAIN
- ↓ DOUBLE CROCHET
- ⋎ INCREASE
- ⋏ DECREASE
- ●— SLIP STITCH

Ⓐ BODY

N 16   Tournesol
N 35   Nacar

ROUND	STITCHES	FORMULA
1	6	◎ 6 ↓
2	12	⋎ × 6
3	18	(⋎ + ↓) × 6
4	24	(⋎ + 2 ↓) × 6
5	30	(⋎ + 3 ↓) × 6
6-7	30	6 ↓ + 24 ↓
8	24	(⋏ + 3 ↓) + (⋏ + 3 ↓) × 5
9-12	24	4 ↓ + 20 ↓
13	18	(⋏ + 2 ↓) × 6
14	18	18 ↓ ●—

BODY

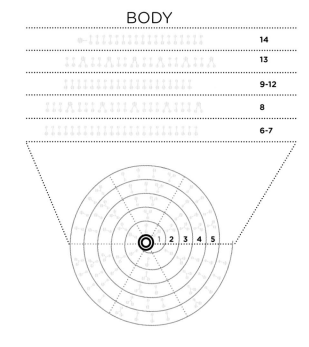

Ⓑ HEAD

N 35 Nacar
◯ N 16 Tournesol

ROUND	STITCHES	FORMULA
1	6	◎ 6 !
2	12	Υ × 6
3	18	(Υ + !) × 6
4	24	(Υ + 2 !) × 6
5	30	(Υ + 3 !) × 6
6	36	(Υ + 4 !) × 6
7-8	36	36 !
9	30	(Λ + 4 !) × 6
10	24	(Λ + 3 !) × 6
11	18	(Λ + 2 !) × 6 ✿ Stuff
12	12	(Λ + !) × 6
13	6	Λ × 6 ←

HEAD

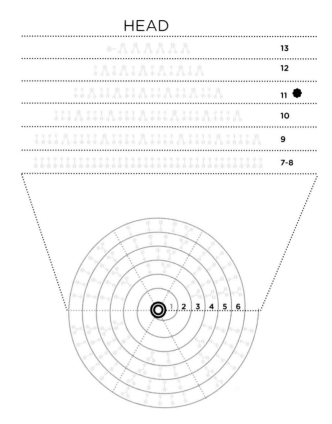

	13
	12
	11 ✿
	10
	9
	7-8

Ⓒ EAR X 2

N 35 Nacar

ROUND	STITCHES	FORMULA
1	6	◎ 6 !
2	6	6 !
3	6	6 ! ←

EAR

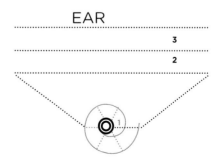

	3
	2
	1

Ⓓ LEG X 4

N 35 Nacar
N 16 Tournesol

ROUND	STITCHES	FORMULA
1	6	◎ 6 !
2	12	Υ × 6
3	12	12 !
4	9	(⅄ + 2 !) × 3
5-10	9	9 !
11	9	9 ! ←

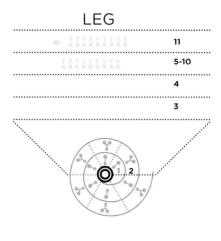

LEG

	11
	5-10
	4
	3

Ⓔ TAIL

N 35 Nacar

ROUND	STITCHES	FORMULA
1	6	◎ 6 ! ←
2-10	6	6 !
11	6	6 ! ←

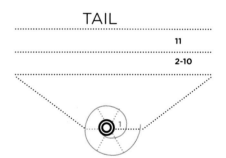

TAIL

| | 11 |
| | 2-10 |

Ⓕ COLLAR

N 14 Green Valley

ROW	STITCHES	FORMULA
1	20	⌐ 20 ◊
2	20	20 ! ←

COLLAR

| | 2 |
| | 1 |

106

ASSEMBLING THE PARTS AND DETAILS

1. Once you have finished all the parts, stuff them.

2. Attach the safety eyes then, close the head.

3. Embroider the mouth using N 11 (Noir) and the nose using N 44 (Agatha).

5. Pin all the parts together.

6. Sew the back legs in a sitting position. Then sew the front legs in a straight down position as shown.

7. Sew the ears to the head then sew the head onto the body.

8. Sew the tail in position.

9. Lastly, wrap the collar around the neck and sew to secure.

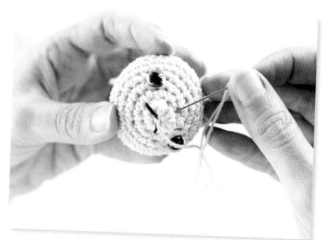

SNOWFLAKE
THE WHITE HORSE

A free spirit who will carry you wherever your heart desires.

YARNS:

DMC NATURA

●	N 37	Canelle
○	N 01	Ibiza
●	N 11	Noir
●	N 41	Siena

MATERIALS:

· Stuffing

· 1 Pair of safety eyes 6 mm

TOOLS:

· 3 mm crochet hook

· Tapestry needle

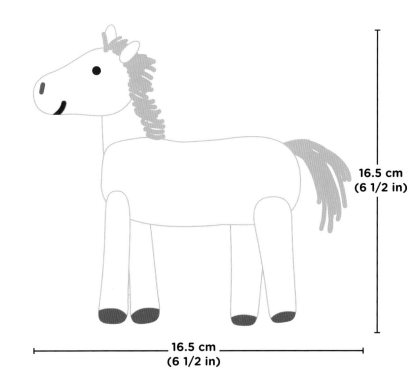

16.5 cm
(6 1/2 in)

16.5 cm
(6 1/2 in)

SNOWFLAKE

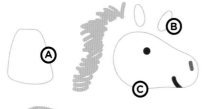
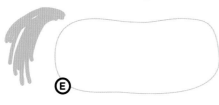
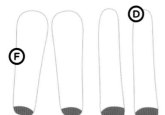

HOW TO CROCHET

Always start with a magic ring of 6 stitches. Work in rounds and finish all the parts of your amigurumi before stuffing them and adding the details.

CHART SYMBOLS

◎ MAGIC RING
� CHAIN STITCH
0 TURNING CHAIN
❗ DOUBLE CROCHET
❣ INCREASE
𝝠 DECREASE
●➤ SLIP STITCH

Ⓑ EAR X 2
N 01   Ibiza

ROUND	STITCHES	FORMULA
1	6	◎ 6❗
2	6	6❗
3	6	6❗ ●➤

EAR

➤ 888888	3
888888	2

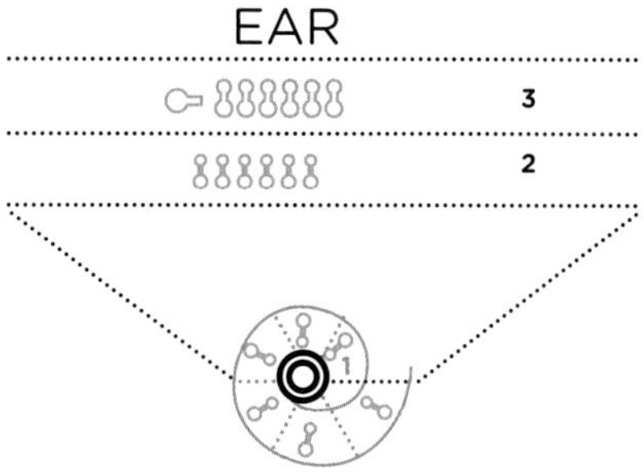

Ⓐ NECK
N 01   Ibiza

ROUND	STITCHES	FORMULA
1	6	◎ 6❗
2	12	❣ x 6
3	18	(❣ + ❗) x 6
4-5	18	❗ 18
6	24	(❣ + 2❗) x 6
7	24	❗ 24
8	24	❗ 24 ●➤

NECK

➤ 8888888888888888888888888	8
888888888888888888888888	7
88❣88❣88❣88❣88❣88❣	6
888888888888888888	4-5

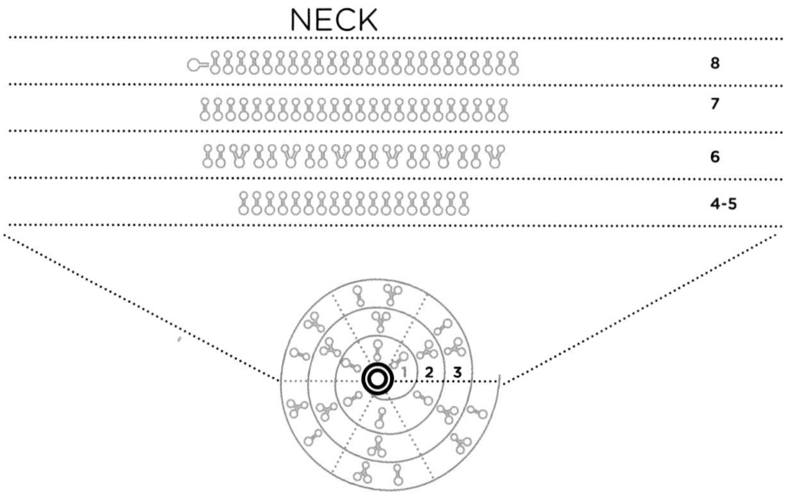

© HEAD

◯ N 01 Ibiza

ROUND	STITCHES	FORMULA
1	6	◎ 6 !
2	12	Y × 6
3	18	(Y + !) × 6
4-8	18	! 18
9	24	(Y + 2 !) × 6
10	30	(Y + 3 !) × 6
11	36	(Y + 4 !) × 6
12	42	(Y + 5 !) × 6
13-14	42	! 42
15	36	(Λ + 5 !) × 6
16	30	(Λ + 4 !) × 6
17	24	(Λ + 3 !) × 6
18	18	(Λ + 2 !) × 6 ❀ Stuff
19	12	(Λ + !) × 6
20	6	Λ + × 6 ←

ⓓ FRONT LEG X 2

⬤ N 41 Siena
◯ N 01 Ibiza

ROUND	STITCHES	FORMULA
1	6	◎ 6 !
2	12	Y × 6
3-4	12	12 !
5-19	12	12 !
20	12	12 ! ←

HEAD

○─ 𝄂𝄂𝄂𝄂𝄂𝄂	20
𝄂𝄂𝄂𝄂𝄂𝄂𝄂𝄂𝄂𝄂𝄂	19
𝄂𝄂𝄂𝄂𝄂𝄂𝄂𝄂𝄂𝄂𝄂𝄂𝄂	18 ❀
𝄂𝄂𝄂𝄂𝄂𝄂𝄂𝄂𝄂𝄂𝄂𝄂𝄂𝄂	17
𝄂𝄂𝄂𝄂𝄂𝄂𝄂𝄂𝄂𝄂𝄂𝄂𝄂𝄂𝄂	16
𝄂𝄂𝄂𝄂𝄂𝄂𝄂𝄂𝄂𝄂𝄂𝄂𝄂𝄂𝄂	15
𝄂𝄂𝄂𝄂𝄂𝄂𝄂𝄂𝄂𝄂𝄂𝄂𝄂𝄂	13-14
𝄂𝄂𝄂𝄂𝄂𝄂𝄂𝄂𝄂𝄂𝄂𝄂	12
𝄂𝄂𝄂𝄂𝄂𝄂𝄂𝄂𝄂𝄂	11
𝄂𝄂𝄂𝄂𝄂𝄂𝄂𝄂	10
𝄂𝄂𝄂𝄂𝄂𝄂	9
𝄂𝄂𝄂𝄂𝄂	4-8

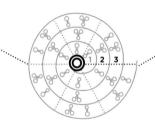

FRONT LEG

○─ 𝄂𝄂𝄂𝄂𝄂𝄂𝄂𝄂𝄂𝄂𝄂	20
𝄂𝄂𝄂𝄂𝄂𝄂𝄂𝄂𝄂𝄂𝄂	5-19
𝄂𝄂𝄂𝄂𝄂𝄂𝄂𝄂𝄂𝄂𝄂	3-4

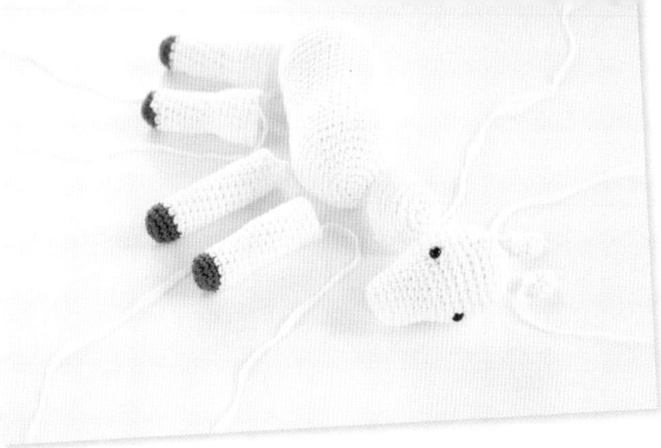

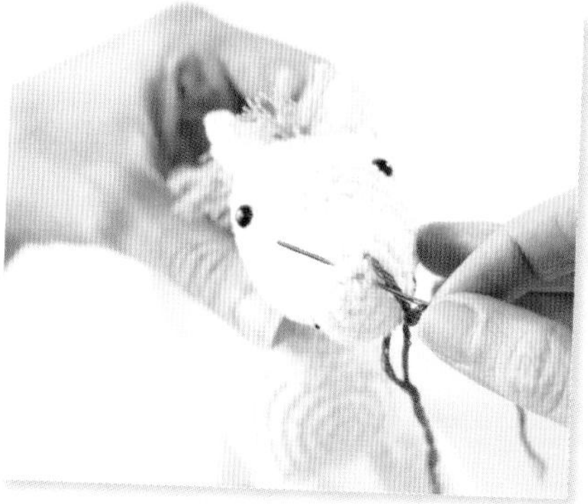

Ⓔ BODY

N 01 Ibiza

ROUND	STITCHES	FORMULA
1	6	◎ 6 !
2	12	Y x 6
3	18	(Y + !) x 6
4	24	(Y + 2 !) x 6
5	30	(Y + 3 !) x 6
6	36	(Y + 4 !) x 6
7	42	(Y + 5 !) x 6
8-11	42	! 42
12	36	(Λ + 5 !) x 6
13-24	36	! 36
25	42	(Y + 5 !) x 6
26-29	42	! 42
30	36	(Λ + 5 !) x 6
31	30	(Λ + 4 !) x 6
32	24	(Λ + 3 !) x 6
33	18	(Λ + 2 !) x 6 ✹ Stuff
34	12	(Λ + !) x 6
35	6	Λ + x 6 •–

BODY

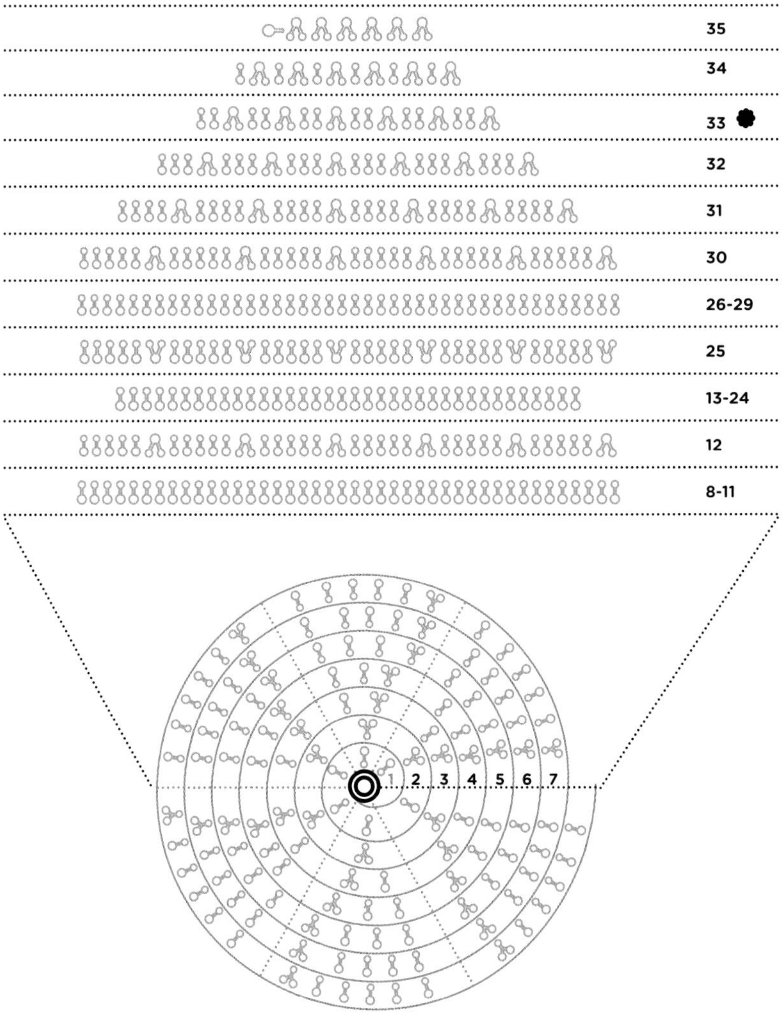

ASSEMBLING THE PARTS AND DETAILS

1. Once you have finished all the parts, stuff them.

2. Attach the safety eyes then close the head.

3. Embroider the mouth using N 11 (Noir) and the nose using N 41 (Siena).

5. Pin all the parts in position.

6. Sew the neck onto the body. Then, sew the ears onto the head and the head onto the neck.

7. Sew the four legs onto the body.

8. Thread a length of N37 (Canelle) onto a needle.

9. Insert the needle into the back at the base of the horse's neck. Knot to secure the yarn then cut it at 2.5cm (1 in) in length. Repeat the process several times over, working up the neck towards the ears, until you have a mane.

10. Do the same for the tail.

Ⓕ HIND LEG X 2

- ● N 41 Siena
- ○ N 01 Ibiza

HIND LEG

	ROUND
↺ 8888888888888888888	20
888888888888888888	16-19
8 8 8 8 8 8 8 8 8 8 8	15
88888888888	5-14
8888888888888	3-4

ROUND	STITCHES	FORMULA
1	6	◎ 6 ⵑ
2	12	Ƴ × 6
3-4	12	12 ⵑ
5-14	12	12 ⵑ
15	18	(Ƴ + ⵑ) × 6
16-19	18	18 ⵑ
20	18	18 ⵑ ⟜

A HAPPY FAMILY
MAKES THE BEST TEAM

Dad, Mom, Son and Daughter ready to play!

YARNS FOR DAD:
DMC NATURA
- N 36 Gardenia
- N 28 Zaphire
- N 41 Siena
- N 22 Tropic Brown
- N 05 Bleu Layette
- N 11 Noir

YARNS FOR MOM:
DMC NATURA
- N 36 Gardenia
- N 22 Tropic Brown
- N 07 Spring Rose
- N 35 Nacar
- N 11 Noir

YARNS FOR DAUGHTER:
DMC NATURA
- N 36 Gardenia
- N 41 Siena
- N 59 Prune
- N 47 Safran
- N 11 Noir

YARNS FOR SON:
DMC NATURA
- N 36 Gardenia
- N 76 Lima
- N 48 Chartreuse
- N 64 Prussian
- N 28 Zaphire
- N 11 Noir

MATERIALS:
- · 2 Pairs of safety eyes 6 mm
- · 2 Pairs of safety eyes 4 mm
- · Stuffing

TOOLS:
- · 3 mm crochet hook
- · Tapestry needle

14 cm
(5 1/2 in)

9.5 cm
(3 3/4 in)

6.5 cm
(2 1/2 in)

3.75 cm
(1 1/2 in)

DAD

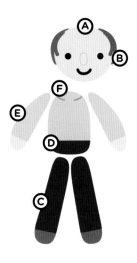

HOW TO CROCHET

Always start with a magic ring of 6 stitches. Work in rounds and finish all the parts of your amigurumi before stuffing them and adding the face details.

CHART SYMBOLS

◎ MAGIC RING
� CHAIN STITCH
0 TURNING CHAIN
❗ DOUBLE CROCHET
Y INCREASE
Λ DECREASE
●– SLIP STITCH

Ⓐ HEAD

N 36 Gardenia

ROUND	STITCHES	FORMULA
1	6	◎ 6 ❗
2	12	Y × 6
3	18	(Y + ❗) × 6
4	24	(Y + 2❗) × 6
5	30	(Y + 3❗) × 6
6	36	(Y + 4❗) × 6
7	42	(Y + 5❗) × 6
8-11	42	❗ 42
12	36	(Λ + 5❗) × 6
13	30	(Λ + 4❗) × 6
14	24	(Λ + 3❗) × 6
15	18	(Λ + 2❗) × 6
16	12	(Λ + ❗) × 6
17	12	❗ 12 ●–

HEAD

	17
	16
	15
	14
	13
	12
	8-11

1 2 3 4 5 6 7

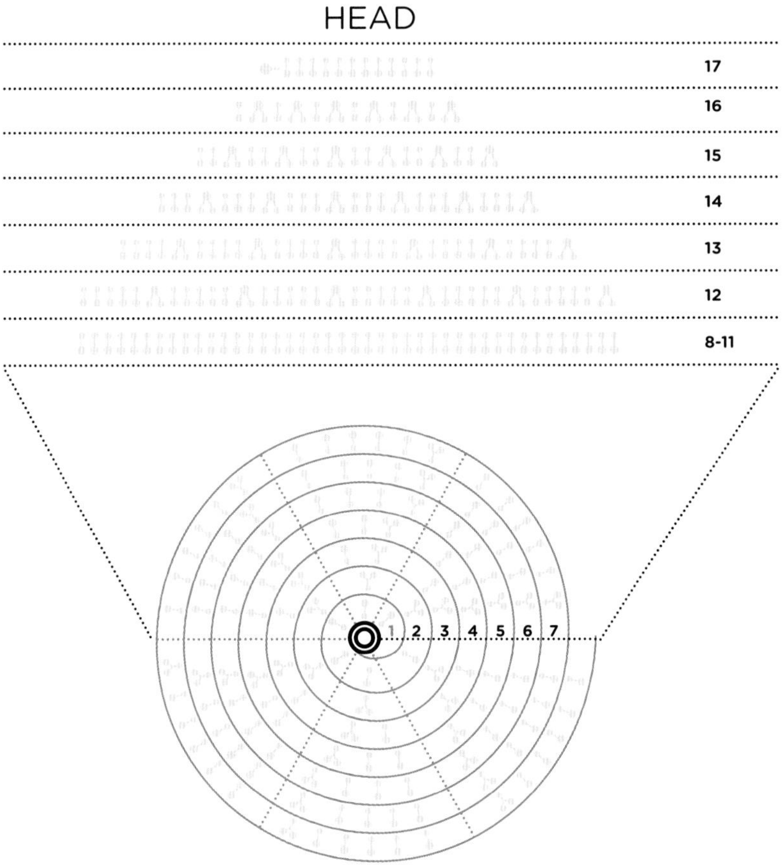

Ⓑ EAR X 2

N 36   Gardenia

ROUND	STITCHES	FORMULA
1	6	◎ 6 ‼️←

EAR

Ⓒ LEG X 2

N 22   Tropic Brown
N 28   Zaphire

ROUND	STITCHES	FORMULA
1	6	◎ 6 ‼
2	12	૪ x 6
3	12	‼ 12
4-16	12	‼ 12
17	12	‼ 12 ←

LEG

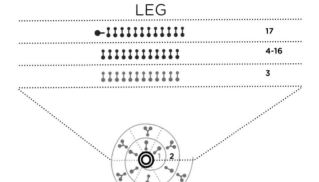

←‼‼‼‼‼‼‼‼‼‼‼‼	17
‼‼‼‼‼‼‼‼‼‼‼‼	4-16
‼‼‼‼‼‼‼‼‼‼‼‼	3

Ⓓ BODY

N 28   Zaphire
N 05   Bleu Layette

ROUND	STITCHES	FORMULA
1	6	◎ 6 ‼
2	12	૪ x 6
3	18	(૪ + ‼) x 6
4	24	(૪ + 2‼) x 6
5-10	24	‼ 24
11	18	(ʌ + 2‼) x 6
12	12	(ʌ + ‼) x 6 ←

BODY

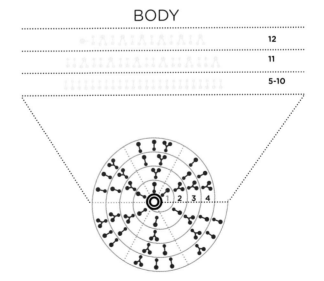

	12
	11
	5-10

Ⓔ ARM X 2

N 36 Gardenia
N 05 Bleu Layette

ROUND	STITCHES	FORMULA
1	6	◎ 6 ¡
2	9	(Υ + ¡) x 3
3-4	9	¡ 9
4-16	9	¡ 9
17	9	¡ 9 ⬤

Ⓕ COLLAR

N 05 Bleu Layette

ROW	STITCHES	FORMULA
1	20	◦ 20 ¡
2	20	20 ¡ ⬤

ARM

●─¡¡¡¡¡¡¡¡¡	17
¡¡¡¡¡¡¡¡¡	4-16
¡¡¡¡¡¡¡¡¡	3-4
Υ¡Υ¡Υ¡	2

COLLAR

●─¡¡¡¡¡¡¡¡¡¡¡¡¡¡¡¡¡¡¡¡	2
◦◦◦◦◦◦◦◦◦◦◦◦◦◦◦◦◦◦◦◦	1

ASSEMBLING THE PARTS AND DETAILS

1. Crochet all the parts.

2. Stuff the head and the body. Then stuff the arms and legs with less stuffing towards the top edges.

3. Attach the safety eyes and sew on the ears.

4. Embroider the nose using N36 (Gardenia) and the mouth using N11 (Noir).

5. Thread a length of N41 (Siena) onto a needle and knot the end.

6. Push the needle through the bottom of the head and out in front of one ear. Sew straight lines all around the back of the head as shown.

7. Repeat until you have covered all around the back of the head.

8. Pin all the parts in position.

9. Sew the head onto the body. Then sew on the arms and legs.

10. Wrap the collar around the neck and sew in place.

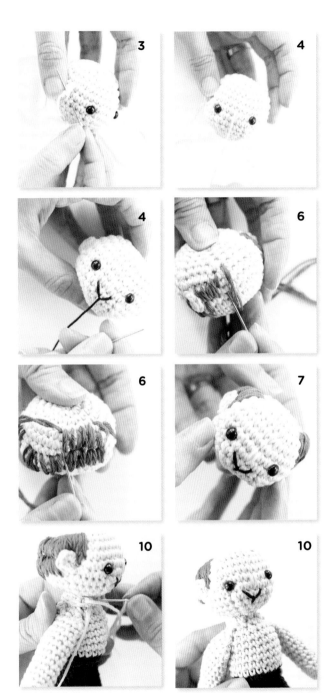

MOM

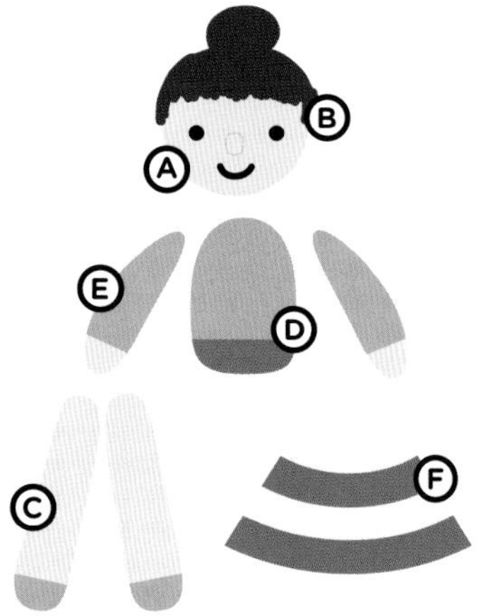

HOW TO CROCHET

Always start with a magic ring of 6 stitches. Work in rounds and finish all the parts of your amigurumi before stuffing them and adding the face details.

CHART SYMBOLS

- ◎ MAGIC RING
- ⬭ CHAIN STITCH
- 0 TURNING CHAIN
- I DOUBLE CROCHET
- Y INCREASE
- Ʌ DECREASE
- •– SLIP STITCH

Ⓐ HEAD

N 36 Gardenia

ROUND	STITCHES	FORMULA
1	6	◎ 6 I
2	12	Y x 6
3	18	(Y + I) x 6
4	24	(Y + 2 I) x 6
5	30	(Y + 3 I) x 6
6	36	(Y + 4 I) x 6
7	42	(Y + 5 I) x 6
8-11	42	I 42
12	36	(Ʌ + 5 I) x 6
13	30	(Ʌ + 4 I) x 6
14	24	(Ʌ + 3 I) x 6
15	18	(Ʌ + 2 I) x 6
16	12	(Ʌ + I) x 6
17	12	I 12 •–

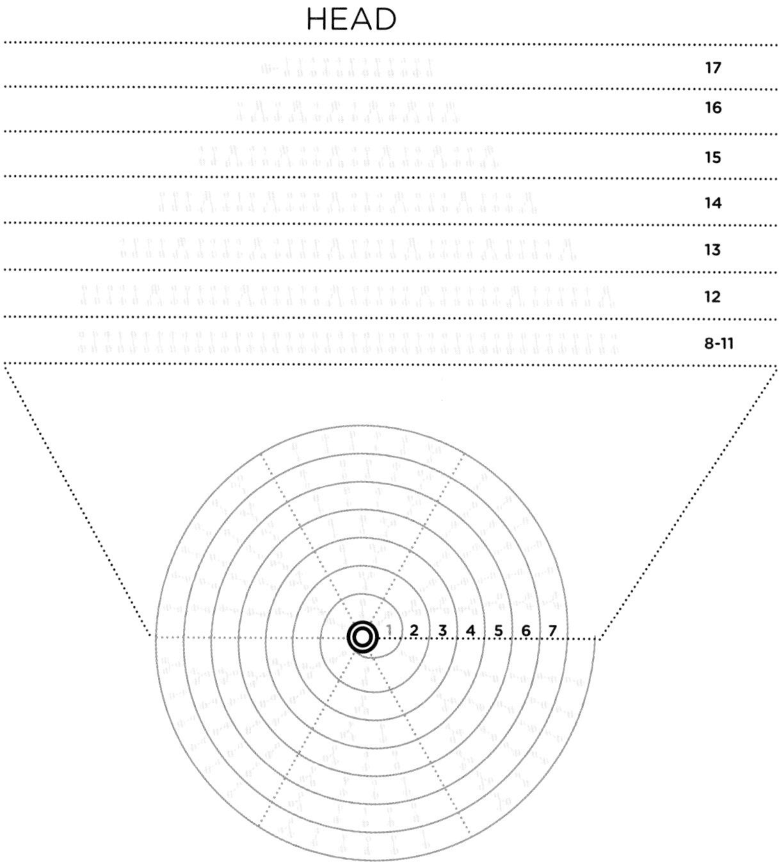

Ⓑ EAR X 2

N 36 Gardenia

ROUND	STITCHES	FORMULA
1	6	◎ 6 ⁑ ←

EAR

ⒸLEG X 2

N 07 Spring Rose
N 36 Gardenia

ROUND	STITCHES	FORMULA
1	6	◎ 6 ⁑
2	12	Υ × 6
3	12	⁑ 12
4-16	12	⁑ 12
17	12	⁑ 12 ←

LEG

⊕-⁑⁑⁑⁑⁑⁑⁑⁑⁑⁑⁑⁑	17
⁑⁑⁑⁑⁑⁑⁑⁑⁑⁑⁑⁑	4-16
⁑⁑⁑⁑⁑⁑⁑⁑⁑⁑⁑⁑	3

ⒹBODY

N 22 Tropic Brown
N 07 Spring Rose

ROUND	STITCHES	FORMULA
1	6	◎ 6 ⁑
2	12	Υ × 6
3	18	(Υ + ⁑) × 6
4	24	(Υ + 2⁑) × 6
5-10	24	⁑ 24
11	18	(Λ + 2⁑) × 6
12	12	(Λ + ⁑) × 6 ←

BODY

●-⁑ΛⁱⁱΛⁱⁱΛⁱⁱΛⁱⁱΛ	12
ⁱⁱΛⁱⁱΛⁱⁱΛⁱⁱΛⁱⁱΛⁱⁱΛ	11
⁑⁑⁑⁑⁑⁑⁑⁑⁑⁑⁑⁑⁑⁑⁑⁑⁑⁑⁑⁑⁑⁑⁑⁑	5-10

Ⓔ ARM X 2

N 36 Gardenia
N 07 Spring Rose

ROUND	STITCHES	FORMULA
1	6	◎ 6 !
2	9	(Υ + !) x 3
3-4	9	! 9
4-16	9	! 9
17	9	! 9 ⊷

Ⓕ SKIRT

N 35 Nacar
N 22 Tropic

Start by making a chain of 24 stitches

ROUND	STITCHES	FORMULA
1	24	⊸ 24 ⊷
2-3	24	! 24
4	30	(Υ + 3 !) x 6
5-6	30	! 30
7	36	(Υ + 4 !) x 6
8-9	36	! 36
10	42	(Υ + 5 !) x 6
11	42	! 42
12	42	! 42 ⊷

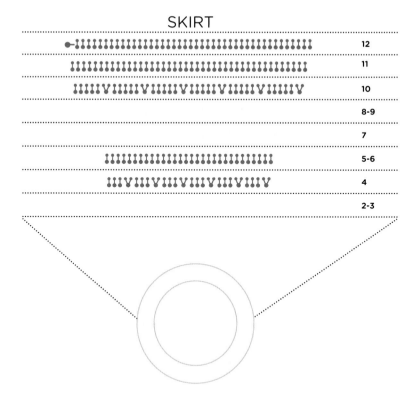

ARM

SKIRT

ASSEMBLING THE PARTS AND DETAILS

1. Crochet all the parts.

2. Stuff the head and the body. Then stuff the arms and legs with less stuffing towards the top edges.

3. Attach the safety eyes and sew on the ears.

4. Embroider the nose using N36 (Gardenia) and the mouth using N11 (Noir).

5. Thread a length of N11 (Noir) onto a needle and knot the end.

6. Push the needle through the bottom of the head and out at centre top. Sew straight lines, towards the centre, all over the top of the head..

7. Then with more N11 (Noir), bring the needle out at the top of the head and sew some loops to make a bun.

8. Pin all the parts in position.

9. Sew the head onto the body. Then sew on the arms and legs.

10. Lastly, sew the top edge of the skirt to the waist of the doll.

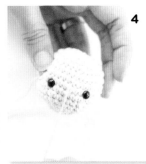

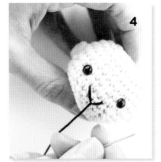

SON & DAUGHTER

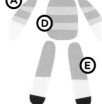

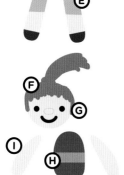

HOW TO CROCHET

Always start with a magic ring of 6 stitches. Work in rounds and finish all the parts of your amigurumi before stuffing them and adding the face details.

CHART SYMBOLS

- ◎ MAGIC RING
- ● CHAIN STITCH
- 0 TURNING CHAIN
- ❚ DOUBLE CROCHET
- ⅄ INCREASE
- ⋀ DECREASE
- ●— SLIP STITCH

HEAD

```
9
8
7
5-6
            1  2  3  4
```

Ⓑ HEAD

N 36 Gardenia

ROUND	STITCHES	FORMULA
1	6	◎ 6 ❚
2	12	⅄ × 6
3	18	(⅄ + ❚) × 6
4	24	(⅄ + 2❚) × 6
5-6	24	❚ 24
7	18	(⋀ + 2❚) × 6
8	12	(⋀ + ❚) × 6
9	12	❚ 12 ●—

ARM

```
●—❚❚❚❚❚❚  8
❚❚❚❚❚❚  7
❚❚❚❚❚❚  6
          2-5
```

Ⓐ ARM X 2

N 36 Gardenia
N 76 Lima
N 48 Chartreuse

ROUND	STITCHES	FORMULA
1	6	◎ 6 ❚
2-5	6	❚ 6
6	6	❚ 6
7	6	❚ 6
8	6	❚ 6 ●—

EAR

Ⓒ EAR X 2

N 36 Gardenia

ROUND	STITCHES	FORMULA
1	4	◎ 4 ❚ ●—

Ⓓ BODY

- N 64 Prussian
- N 76 Lima
- N 48 Chartreuse

ROUND	STITCHES	FORMULA
1	6	◎ 6 ‡
2	12	Υ × 6
3	18	(Υ + ‡) × 6
4	18	‡ 18
5	18	‡ 18
6	18	‡ 18
7	18	‡ 18
8	12	(Λ + ‡) × 6 ←

BODY

●‡Λ‡Λ‡Λ‡Λ‡Λ‡Λ‡	8
‡‡‡‡‡‡‡‡‡‡‡‡‡‡‡‡‡‡	7
‡‡‡‡‡‡‡‡‡‡‡‡‡‡‡‡‡‡	6
‡‡‡‡‡‡‡‡‡‡‡‡‡‡‡‡‡‡	4-5
‡‡‡‡‡‡‡‡‡‡‡‡‡‡‡‡‡‡	

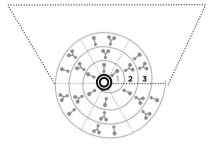

Ⓔ LEG X2

- N 28 Zaphire
- N 36 Gardenia
- N 64 Prussian

ROUND	STITCHES	FORMULA
1	6	◎ 6 ‡
2	9	(Υ + ‡) × 3
3	9	‡ 9
4-7	9	‡ 9
8-9	9	‡ 9
10	9	‡ 9 ←

LEG

●‡‡‡‡‡‡‡‡‡	10
‡‡‡‡‡‡‡‡‡	8-9
‡‡‡‡‡‡‡‡‡	4-7
‡‡‡‡‡‡‡‡‡	3
‡Υ‡Υ‡Υ	2

Ⓕ HEAD

- N 36 Gardenia

ROUND	STITCHES	FORMULA
1	6	◎ 6 ‡
2	12	Υ × 6
3	18	(Υ + ‡) × 6
4	24	(Υ + 2‡) × 6
5-6	24	‡ 24
7	18	(Λ + 2‡) × 6
8	12	(Λ + ‡) × 6
9	12	‡ 12 ←

Ⓖ EAR X 2

- N 36 Gardenia

ROUND	STITCHES	FORMULA
1	4	◎ 4 ‡ ←

HEAD

●‡‡‡‡‡‡‡‡‡‡	9
‡‡‡‡‡‡‡‡‡‡‡‡	8
‡‡‡‡‡‡‡‡‡‡‡‡‡‡	7
‡‡‡‡‡‡‡‡‡‡‡‡‡‡‡‡	5-6

EAR

125

Ⓗ BODY

- ⬤ N 59 Prune
- ⬤ N 47 Safran

ROUND	STITCHES	FORMULA
1	6	◎ 6 ꭝ
2	12	⅄ × 6
3	18	(⅄ + ꭝ) × 6
4	18	ꭝ 18
5-7	18	ꭝ 18
8	12	(⋀ + ꭝ) × 6 ◂

BODY

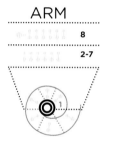

◂ ꭝ ⋀ ꭝ ⋀ ꭝ ⋀ ꭝ ⋀ ꭝ ⋀	8
ꭝꭝꭝꭝꭝꭝꭝꭝꭝꭝꭝꭝꭝꭝꭝꭝꭝꭝ	5-7
ꭝꭝꭝꭝꭝꭝꭝꭝꭝꭝꭝꭝꭝꭝꭝꭝꭝꭝ	4

Ⓘ ARM X2

- ⬤ N 36 Gardenia

ROUND	STITCHES	FORMULA
1	6	◎ 6 ꭝ
2-7	6	ꭝ 6
8	6	ꭝ 6 ◂

ARM

⬦⎯ꭝꭝꭝꭝꭝꭝ	8
ꭝꭝꭝꭝꭝꭝ	2-7

Ⓙ LEG X2

- ⬤ N 47 Safran
- ⬤ N 36 Gardenia

ROUND	STITCHES	FORMULA
1	6	◎ 6 ꭝ
2	9	(⅄ + ꭝ) × 3
3	9	ꭝ 9
4-9	9	ꭝ 9
10	9	ꭝ 9 ◂

LEG

⬦⎯ꭝꭝꭝꭝꭝꭝ	10
ꭝꭝꭝꭝꭝꭝ	4-9
ꭝꭝꭝꭝꭝꭝꭝꭝꭝ	3
ꭝ⅄ꭝ⅄ꭝ⅄	2

SKIRT

◂ ꭝꭝꭝꭝꭝꭝꭝꭝꭝꭝꭝꭝꭝꭝꭝꭝꭝꭝꭝꭝꭝꭝꭝꭝꭝ	5
ꭝꭝV ꭝꭝV ꭝꭝV ꭝꭝV ꭝꭝV ꭝꭝV	4
ꭝꭝꭝꭝꭝꭝꭝꭝꭝꭝꭝꭝꭝꭝꭝꭝꭝꭝ	2-3

Ⓚ SKIRT

- ⬤ N 59 Prune

Start by making a chain of 18 stitches

ROUND	STITCHES	FORMULA
1	18	◦ 18 ◂
2-3	18	ꭝ 18
4	24	(⅄ + 2 ꭝ) × 6
5	24	ꭝ 24 ◂

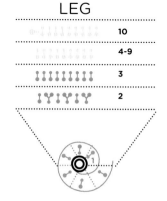

ASSEMBLING THE PARTS AND DETAILS

1. Crochet all the parts.

2. Stuff the head and the body. Then stuff the arms and legs with less stuffing towards the top edges.

3. Attach the safety eyes and sew on the ears.

4. Embroider the nose using N36 (Gardenia) and the mouth using N11 (Noir).

5. To make the daughter's hair: thread a length of N41 (Siena) onto a needle and knot the end.

6. Push the needle through the bottom of the head and out at centre top. Sew straight lines, towards the centre, all over the top of the head.

7. To make the ponytail: with more yarn, bring the needle out at the top of the head and make a knot close to the head then cut the yarn leaving a 2.5cm (1 in) tail. Repeat several times to make a bunch.

8. To make the son's hair: thread a length of N11 (Noir) onto a needle and knot the end.

9. Push the needle through the bottom of the head and out at one side on the top. Sew straight lines, from this side point, all over the top of the head.

10. Pin all the parts in position.

11. Sew the head onto the body. Then sew on the arms and legs.

12. Lastly, sew the top edge of the skirt to the waist of the daughter.

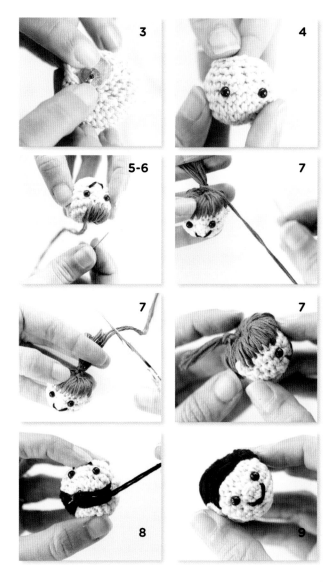

DMC NATURA COLOUR PALETTE

In this book we only use DMC Natura Just Cotton,
here you can see the complete range of 60 colours.

N 01	Ibiza	N 26	Blue Jeans	N 30	Glicine
N 02	Ivory	N 28	Zaphire	N 88	Orléans
N 35	Nacar	N 27	Star Light	N 31	Malva
N 36	Gardenia	N 53	Blue Night	N 59	Prune
N 37	Canelle	N 49	Turquoise	N 45	Orquidea
N 78	Lin	N 64	Prussian	N 44	Agatha
N 39	Ombre	N 54	Green Smoke	N 80	Salomé
N 22	Tropic Brown	N 14	Green Valley	N 03	Sable
N 41	Siena	N 46	Forêt	N 83	Blé
N 86	Brique	N 38	Liquen	N 16	Tournesol
N 85	Giroflée	N 81	Acanthe	N 75	Moss Green
N 47	Safran	N 82	Lobelia	N 43	Golden Lemon
N 18	Coral	N 52	Geranium	N 74	Curry
N 23	Passion	N 07	Spring Rose	N 12	Light Green
N 34	Bourgogne	N 06	Rose Layette	N 79	Tilleul
N 87	Glacier	N 32	Rose Soraya	N 76	Bamboo
N 20	Jade	N 51	Erica	N 13	Pistache
N 25	Aguamarina	N 33	Amaranto	N 48	Chartreuse
N 05	Bleu Layette	N 62	Cerise	N 09	Gris Argent
N 56	Azur	N 61	Crimson	N 11	Noir